LITTLE BOXES

Little Boxes is one of the most effective double bills recently staged in London. Both the one-act plays that go to make it up portray people living isolated lives in city flats. *The Coffee Lace* concerns three married couples who between them make up a retired variety act and its long-suffering manager, Johnny. They eke out an impoverished existence, living off memories, the occasional drama lesson, and the lost property found on the underground by Johnny – the only member of the household who ever goes out. In *Trevor*, one of two girls in their late twenties, who live together as lovers in a smart flat, is faced with a visit from her parents and invites an actor to tea to play the role of the fiancé they think she ought to have. Unfortunately two sets of parents descend simultaneously and 'Trevor' finds himself playing a double role.

'After laughing oneself silly one is suddenly bemused with thought. *Little Boxes* confirms the feeling created by Mr Bowen's *I Love You, Mrs Patterson* and *After the Rain* that a major talent, disturbing, brooding and despite its humour, essentially tragic, has come into the British theatre.'

Harold Hobson in the *Sunday Times*

John Bowen

LITTLE BOXES:

THE COFFEE LACE
TREVOR

LONDON
METHUEN & CO LTD
11 NEW FETTER LANE EC4

First published 1968
© 1968 by John Bowen

This book is available in both hardbound and paperback editions.

Printed in Great Britain by
COX & WYMAN LTD.,
LONDON, READING AND FAKENHAM

For
DAVID COOK

CONTENTS

AUTHOR'S NOTE

These plays are designed as a double bill. They are both plays about people who live in boxes. In the first play, the people are old, and they get out. In the second, they are young, and are shut in.

The set for both plays should be identical in shape, but differently dressed in each case, since the people of the first play are poor, and those of the second are comfortably situated. The same actors should play in each play. Any company performing the first play, should adapt the details of Johnny's underground foraging to suit the town or city in which the play is performed, using its own metro system, bus routes, and the characteristics of the people who live in its own various districts. Similarly in the second play, the Chelsea Breather can change his place of operation, and Trevor need not live in Paulton's Square.

The plays were first performed at the Hampstead Theatre Club, and then at the Duchess Theatre. Once the set was placed on the Hampstead stage, there was no wing space. The Duchess had wing space but an even smaller stage between the two sides of the proscenium arch, and no apron. Consequently *The Coffee Lace* had to be a little revised to fit these stages, and in particular it lost its original ending. In this text I indicate how the play should be played in theatres with an apron stage.

The Coffee Lace

Little Boxes was first performed at the Hampstead Theatre Club on February 26th, 1968. The cast of *The Coffee Lace* was as follows:

LILY	June Jago
MR DAVIS	David Cook
SONNY	Frank Middlemass
IRIS	Maureen Pryor
ROSE	Sylvia Coleridge
JIMMY	Larry Noble
JOHNNY	Peter Howell
MADGE	Angela Thorne
MISS PEEL	Anna Cropper

Both *The Coffee Lace* and *Trevor* were directed by Philip Grout, and designed by J. Hutchinson Scott.

On April 1st, 1968, *Little Boxes* transferred to the Duchess Theatre. The part of Madge was there played by Elizabeth MacClennan.

SCENE ONE

The stage shows the top-floor flat of a decayed Victorian house. There are three rooms and a lavatory. The smallest of the three rooms is at a higher level than the others, and is reached by a short winding staircase, opening off the passage that runs the full depth of the stage, and divides the largest room (stage left) from the two others. This is the room belonging to LILY *and* JOHNNY: *it has a kitchen alcove screened off at the back.* SONNY *and* IRIS *live on the same level, their door opening directly opposite that of* LILY's *room, separated only by the passage.* ROSE *and* JIMMY *live in the small room upstairs. Only the lavatory door is seen: it is at the upstage end of the passage. Next to it, but opening to the right off the passage, is the door to the downstairs world. Each room has a double bed, but the two smaller rooms are otherwise sparsely furnished.* LILY *and* JOHNNY's *room is also the common room for the three couples. It is the only one with a gas-fire in it. Each of the other rooms has a small round, portable electric fire, giving little heat.*

When the curtain rises, ROSE *and* JIMMY *are sitting crouched over their fire. One wears an eiderdown over day-clothes, the other a blanket, and both wear woolly gloves.* IRIS *and* SONNY *are over the fire in their rooms. Both wear overcoats.* SONNY *is stitching tinselly braid to a blouse.* LILY *is in bed. The gas-fire is full on.* LILY *is giving a lesson to* MR DAVIS, *the young man from the pawnshop.* MR DAVIS *wishes to become an actor, but has been persuaded that he needs coaching before applying to one of the acting schools for an audition.*

The rooms, the clothes, the furniture are worn and shabby. What photographs and bric-a-brac there are give evidence of a theatrical past before the 1939-45 war. The time is a day in February.

Unless indicated, the characters in those rooms where action is not, for the time being, concentrated, simply sit still.

All the occupants of this flat are in their sixties, ROSE *the youngest,* LILY *the oldest. Only* MR DAVIS *is young, but he is from the world outside.*

Light fades up in each room in turn as the characters speak.

ROSE. It's cold. It's very cold here. We've got the draughty room. We've always had it.

IRIS. You get no heat from one bar. None. You might as well have it off.

LILY. When ugly people fall in love, it is never with other ugly people. One might think it more suitable if they did, but they do not.

DAVIS. Yes, Miss Terralozzi.

LILY. Luckily beautiful people seldom fall in love with anyone at all, so they may as well marry ugly people. That is why I married Mr Sims.

DAVIS. The vicar had a word with me.

LILY. You have a gap in your teeth, Mr Davis.

DAVIS. He wondered if you'd consent to appear at the Senior Citizens Evening.

LILY. A gap. A distinct gap.

DAVIS. Songs and dramatic recitations. With Old Time Dancing after, but you'd not be expected to join in. There'd be a fee. Two guineas, the vicar said.

LILY. We never go out. You know that.

DAVIS. But it's a professional engagement, Miss Terralozzi. There's a special Fund to cover it in Church Expenses. The Senior Citizens Entertainment Fund.

LILY. Two guineas?

DAVIS. Yes.

LILY. Eight and sixpence each. Please inform the vicar that artistes of our standing do not appear for eight and sixpence. Meanwhile, you have a gap in your teeth. You must have it filled. I spoke of this at our last lesson.

DAVIS. You always speak of it.

LILY. For an artiste, a good appearance is half the battle. More than half. I've known people in the profession who had nothing else.

DAVIS. I went to the dentist.

LILY. Excellent.

DAVIS. He said it'd cost me.

LILY. What?

DAVIS. Money, Miss Terralozzi.

LILY. Is there no National Health?

DAVIS. Not for cosmetics. He said if it's not for chewing, it's cosmetic.

LILY. Then you must use the teeth that come into your pawn-shop.

DAVIS. They wouldn't fit me. You have to have them fitted. Anyway nobody pawns teeth nowadays.

LILY. Nonsense. It's well known that the poor pawn their teeth. (*Calls.*) Iris!

ROSE *and* JIMMY *look at each other. So do* SONNY *and* IRIS.

SONNY. She wants you.

IRIS. Showing off. She wants to show off. She wants to show she can call me, and I come.

LILY (*calls*). Iris, dear!

IRIS *gets up, takes off her overcoat, then crosses the hall to* LILY's *room, and enters.*

Iris, do the poor pawn their teeth?

IRIS. Is that why you called?

LILY. Mr Davis was asking. He has an interest.

IRIS. I've known it done. I've heard of it.

LILY (*to* DAVIS). Miss Fellowes comes of a very poor home. She knows these things.

DAVIS. Yes, Miss Terralozzi.

LILY. In Miss Fellowes' day, many of us in the profession were born into poverty. It was no disgrace, you understand. Miss Fellowes raised herself.

IRIS. If you've finished the lesson, we'll come in by the fire where it's warm.

LILY. You have your own fire.

IRIS. It's getting dark in there. Grey. You can't have the fire and the light both on, you know that.

LILY (*looking at* DAVIS). Please, Iris, dear. Please. (*To* DAVIS.) What is the time, Mr Davis?

DAVIS. I've only had forty-five minutes.

LILY. I shall not cheat you. (*To* IRIS.) In fifteen minutes, Miss Fellowes.

IRIS. I could stay and hear him with you. (*To* DAVIS, *who is alarmed*.) You'd benefit from an audience.

LILY. I shall decide when Mr Davis is ready to expose himself to the public, Miss Fellowes. (*Indicates the door*.) If you please.

IRIS hesitates, and goes out. She crosses the hall to her own room.

IRIS. She's got that fire going full blast. She doesn't need it. She's in bed. She has the body warmth.

SONNY. The boy needs it.

IRIS. He has his overcoat. He can wear that. Five shillings an hour! Anyone else would charge a pound.

SONNY. We have to keep him sweet, dear. We have to keep that boy sweet. He gave us three pound on your cameo brooch. I don't know how he explains it to Mr Simon.

IRIS. It was worth six.

SONNY. No, dear, not that brooch. Not six.

IRIS. I wore that brooch all through *The Dollar Princess*. I wore it in the Garden Party scene in Act Two.

SONNY. Just the same dear, you know as well as I do, you picked it up for half a crown at a totter's in Greenwich.

Return to the main room.

LILY. For a while, we had an act of our own, you know. The Three Posies, with Sonny and Jim. My husband managed it.

IRIS. We should go in. Ridiculous. Wasting the fire.

DAVIS. I never see your husband.

IRIS. He learns nothing.

LILY. You see him in the shop.

DAVIS. Yes, he comes to the shop sometimes. But, I mean, he's not here, is he? I don't meet him.

LILY. Mr Sims goes out a great deal. His work takes him to the City.

DAVIS. Ah . . .

LILY. Mr Sims deals with the business side of things.

DAVIS. That's right. I give him three pound on a cameo brooch.

LILY. In the profession, Mr Davis, we are not expected to know about the business side. Mr Sims had money of his own when I married him. He had a private income. Miss Fellowes and Miss Deveraux married within the profession, but that was not at all usual. It shows a lack of self-respect. In Miss Deveraux, I could understand it. She was never serious. We are all very fond of Miss Deveraux here, but she has been a frivolous little thing all her life, and it does no good to deny it. She might have married a specialist in Nervous Diseases at the Charing Cross Hospital, but, as one might expect, she gave too much too soon.

DAVIS. I'm nervous myself, Miss Terralozzi. I've always been nervous, as a matter of fact. That's why I want to go on the stage.

LILY. Mr Sims used to come to *Dancing with Daisy* at least three times a week. He booked a stall for the run, always the same stall. And when *I* appeared, he would burst into spontaneous applause.

IRIS. She's never been a true professional. We should take it in turns, teaching him. Then we'd have the fire.

DAVIS. My mother said . . .

LILY. Yes?

DAVIS. She was listening to *Woman's Hour* on the wireless. There was this lady talking about dramatic movement.

LILY. What *about* dramatic movement?

DAVIS. She said they had evening classes at the Polytechnic. She said I ought to go.

Pause.

LILY. Do you suggest we overcharge you here?

DAVIS. No . . . No. Five bob an hour: it's very reasonable.

LILY. We do it as a favour.

DAVIS. Yes.

LILY. You find me unsympathetic then?

DAVIS. No.

LILY. Incompetent? You have lost faith in my coaching.

DAVIS (*desperate*). But you don't teach me *movement*.

SONNY. We have to keep him sweet, that boy. It's important. With the anniversary coming up, I don't know what we should do.

IRIS. We've nothing to pawn.

SONNY. There's the coffee lace.

LILY (*calls, not loud*). Miss Fellowes!

IRIS. She won't part with it.

LILY (*calls*). Miss Fellowes.

Reactions from ROSE *and* JIMMY *upstairs,* IRIS *and* SONNY *across the hall.*

IRIS. I won't be called twice in an hour. It's too much. I shan't go.

JIMMY *opens the door of the upstairs room, and listens.*

JIMMY. It's Iris. She wants Iris again.

ROSE. She goes too far. We're not servants.

DAVIS. Shall I go and knock on the door? She may be deaf.

LILY. She is not deaf. She is in excellent health. (*Calls.*) Miss Fellowes!

SONNY *gives* IRIS *a look.*

SONNY. Go on, dear.

IRIS *goes into the main room, while:*

ROSE. What is it?

JIMMY. She wants Iris again. She's calling Iris.

ROSE. If it's important, we should all go.

JIMMY. She'll call if it's important.

IRIS. Well?

LILY. Mr Davis wishes to be taught dramatic movement.

DAVIS. I thought . . . If I could feel at ease.

IRIS (*to* DAVIS). You've got a gap in your teeth, do you know that? You get that fixed, if you want to feel at ease. I mean, it stands to reason; you're self-conscious, aren't you?

DAVIS. I thought . . . If I could move dramatically.

IRIS. You can't keep moving all the time. They're bound to notice it, the moment you stop.

LILY. I'd deal with it myself, but I am ill, as you know.

IRIS. Indigestion!

LILY (*warns*). Iris!

IRIS (*to* DAVIS). She gets pains in her stomach, and calls it illness.

LILY (*control*). The pains in my upper abdomen are nothing to do with Mr Davis, dear. He is not a medical man.

IRIS (*to* DAVIS). Pains! You see that hand? (*Shows it.*) On a wet day, it takes me five minutes to straighten the fingers. I've cried – cried with that hand.

LILY. Iris –

IRIS (*to* LILY). And Sonny with his kidneys, standing there in the toilet for half an hour together.

LILY. Iris!

IRIS. You could get up out of that bed, and take Mr Davis into our room for his lessons. He's got his overcoat. He doesn't need the fire. It's wind: that's all it is. You get wind, and call it pains, and we suffer.

LILY (*thunder*). I am to have tests for my pains.

Both JIMMY *upstairs and* SONNY, *with the door open in the next room, hear this.* SONNY *stands up, and comes to the hall during the pause which follows. Then:*

DAVIS. I better go. (*Pause.*) I've had my hour. I've learned a lot.

In the hall, SONNY *makes up his mind to go in. He squares his shoulders, and makes an entrance. Lots of attack.*

SONNY. Hullo, dears. Hullo, Mr Davis, dear. Enjoying yourself, are you? That's right.

DAVIS. I've just finished.

LILY. I asked your wife for assistance with –

IRIS. You never asked. You said you were ill. That's all.

LILY. She became unpleasant over my pains.

IRIS. I was cold.

LILY. Mr Davis required help.

SONNY. What sort of help?

DAVIS. I thought . . . with dramatic movement.

SONNY. Dancing! We can do that. Sonny Lynn and Iris
Fellowes – we could teach him the elements. Tap. Soft-shoe.
(*To* DAVIS.) Not ballet. We didn't *do* ballet. You've got a
gap in your teeth, Mr Davis, dear. You ought to have it
fixed. No, we did a lot with canes. We did formation dancing.
We never did ballet.

DAVIS. There was a lady did it on the wireless.

SONNY (*takes his arm and leads him into the corridor and then
into the other room*). So she may, so she may, Mr Davis dear,
but if you can't see her, you don't know if she's doing it right.
Come along, Iris dear, we'll just go into the other room with
the piano, and teach Mr Davis a little routine. Then he can
practise at home in front of a mirror.

IRIS (*to* LILY). We'll need the light on in the other room.
(*Goes over to the gas-fire and switches it out.*) You know the
rule.

LILY. But I'm an invalid. I require care.

IRIS. If you've got a temperature, you don't need the fire.
(*Calls.*) You can turn the light on, Sonny. The fire's out here.

SONNY *turns on the light, and opens the lid of the piano.*

SONNY. Now isn't that cosy, Mr Davis dear. But you'd better
keep your coat on till we warm you up.

IRIS *goes through to the other room.*

DAVIS. I didn't know you had a piano.

SONNY. You would if we lived on the ground floor, Mr Davis
dear. You'd have had it in your pawnshop. (*Finds the song:
to* IRIS.) Iris dear, you remember this?

IRIS (*takes the music*). You don't expect me to play the piano
with my arthritis.

SONNY. I wasn't asking you to play, dear. Just if you remem-
bered it. (*To* DAVIS.) You'll enjoy this one, Mr Davis dear.
(*Note on the piano.*) There's the note.

Upstairs, JIMMY *and* ROSE *have been listening.*

ROSE. They're playing the piano.

JIMMY. They're never.

ROSE. I heard it.

JIMMY. They're not playing now.

ROSE. Listen, cleversticks.

Back to the lesson.

SONNY. I'm going to teach you something very simple to start with, Mr Davis dear.

DAVIS. Movement?

SONNY. That's right, dear, simple movement. We'll do one two three kick, and then back.

DAVIS. Back.

SONNY. And then one two three kick again. I'll do it with you, and Iris will sing. Unless you'd rather play the piano, Iris dear. Do your *fingers* good.

IRIS. I'll sing.

SONNY. Right. With me. (*Points out front.*) There's the audience. Smile, Mr Davis dear. Big smile.

IRIS (*sings*). Over my	SONNY. One two three
shoulder goes	Out you go
one care	Back now.
Over my	One two three
shoulder go	Kick again.
two cares –	That's right.

ROSE. Iris is singing.

JIMMY. That's the television next door.

ROSE. I'm going down.

JIMMY. They'll think you want something.

ROSE. Well, I do. I want to know what's going on.

ROSE *begins to come down.* JIMMY *stays where he is.* SONNY *now goes on with the routine, the first two lines having been repeated in silence during the last five lines.*

SONNY. You're not knock-kneed, Mr Davis dear, are you?

DAVIS *shakes his head, still smiling.*

No? Well, that's very good. Very good indeed. Now we'll do the next two. Iris?

ROSE *enters the room.*

ROSE. Has he gone?

DAVIS. Good evening, Miss Deveraux. We're doing dramatic movement.

ROSE (*to* SONNY). He's got a gap in his teeth. Someone should tell him.

SONNY. We have, dear; we all have. Come along, Mr Davis dear. Watch me. Iris?

IRIS *sings the next two lines, and* SONNY *bends his knees in time to the music, watched by* ROSE *and* DAVIS.

Do you think you could do that, Mr Davis dear. Rose dear, I finished your blouse. It's on the table.

ROSE (*gets it*). Oh, Sonny, you are good to me.

IRIS. Are we going on or aren't we?

ROSE (*showing to* DAVIS). Isn't that nice, Mr Davis? Isn't it lovely.

DAVIS. Very attractive.

ROSE. I've always liked bright colours. You can wear bright colours or you can't. Something glittery; I can't resist it.

IRIS (*sings*). *Why* should I –

ROSE. No, Iris. He can't get the beat with you singing. He needs the piano.

IRIS. I'm not playing the piano with my arth –

ROSE. Nobody's asking you, Iris. We wouldn't expect it. Jimmy can play. (*Goes to the door and calls.*) Jimmy! Come down, you're wanted.

JIMMY. If I'm wanted, I'll come.

ROSE (*as he descends*). You're to play the piano.

LILY, *unable to bear this, has got out of bed. She goes to the door of her room, hesitates with her hand on the handle, then changes her mind. She goes to the wardrobe, and gets a large old-fashioned hat with a ribbon. She tries it on, in front of the mirror.*

SONNY. Come along, Jimmy dear. You know the tune. Give him the music, Iris dear. Now, Mr Davis dear, we'll do it together. Rose, dear. Iris. All together. We're the boys, Mr Davis dear, and they're the girls. Jimmy!

JIMMY *begins to play, and the three perform their routine, along with* DAVIS.

The routine is repeated, DAVIS *encouraged. In the other room,* LILY *takes the centre of the stage, prepares herself, then begins a routine of her own. So we have four and the piano in one room,* LILY *dancing and singing by herself in a big hat in the other.*

The door from downstairs opens. JOHNNY *enters. He is wearing an overcoat, very worn. He carries a bundle of papers and magazines. He comes into the corridor, stops on hearing the noise, listens. Then he opens the door to the large room quietly.*

LILY *does not see him. She continues to sing and dance. As she reaches the end of the chorus, she strikes an attitude.*

SONNY (*breathless*). Very nice, Mr Davis dear. You do pick things up.

JOHNNY *applauds.* LILY *turns to see him. She takes a step towards him. Then the pain hits her – a sharp pain in the upper stomach.*

LILY. Pain.

In the next room, a freeze. From now on, the coaching of DAVIS *will continue only intermittently and as indicated, freezing into a still picture when it is not wanted.*

JOHNNY *has put down his bundle of papers in order to applaud. Now he helps* LILY *to sit on the bed.*

JOHNNY. Tum-tum, is it?

LILY *nods.*

(*Feels in his pocket*). Brought you some Settlers.

As she takes one, the music starts again next door. First two lines sung and danced. Then freeze.

Rehearsing?

LILY. They are teaching Mr Davis dramatic movement.

SONNY. Smile, Mr Davis dear. Big smile. That's right.

LILY. Sonny says we should keep him sweet in view of the anniversary.

JOHNNY. Yes. (*Pause.*) That's true, dammit. (*Pause.*) Oh damn, and blast, and hell.

LILY. You were not successful?

JOHNNY. No luck. No luck at all. I go out every morning, and come back with nothing but mags. Nothing we can sell.

LILY. You must not doubt yourself, Johnny. If *you* were to doubt, we should all surrender.

JOHNNY. I could be here, looking after you, instead of riding round and round on a damned underground train, hoping to find lost property. (*Pause.*) Lil . . .

LILY. Yes?

JOHNNY. Old doctor came, eh?

LILY. I am to have tests. I told Iris so, but she is a grudging woman. You should not have brought home the *Reader's Digest*. Since reading it she has become a medical authority. Indigestion! 'I might have an ulcer,' I said to her, 'And where would you all be then without my leadership?'

JOHNNY. It's not an ulcer, Lil.

LILY. Why should it not be?

JOHNNY. Too high up. My old dad had an ulcer. Bound to, I suppose, working on the Stock Exchange. And then *I* was a worry to him. Used to get this gnawing pain before meals. Everything boiled, and no lettuce. Ghastly life.

LILY. Well, I am to have tests.

Pause. JOHNNY *finds difficulty in looking at her.*

JOHNNY. He didn't give you any idea what sort of tests?

LILY. It is not cancer, Johnny, if that is what you fear.

Next room, music: 'Why should I care,' etc. ROSE *does a little dance of her own. Applause.*

ROSE. We'll have to stop. I'm quite out of breath.

SONNY. He's very good, isn't he? You're very good, Mr Davis dear. Picks it up very quickly. It's all right, Mr Davis dear; you can stop smiling now.

JIMMY. He's got a gap in his teeth. He'll never make a juvenile.

SONNY. Never mind, dear. Never *mind*, Jimmy dear.

JIMMY (*to* DAVIS). Comedy; that should be your aim. You should do comedy. Shouldn't he do comedy, Rosie?

SONNY. We'll teach him comedy next week.

IRIS. One thing at a time.

DAVIS. I wouldn't mind doing comedy.

JIMMY. I'll teach you. Comic patter. Jokes. Falling. We'll go into the big room with the fire . . .

ROSE. I don't want you to fall, Jimmy. I don't want you to do falling.

SONNY. He'll do the falling dear. Jimmy won't fall.

DAVIS. That's right. I don't mind falling.

ROSE. Well, you're not to let my husband fall. He's got bones like a bird, very fine and brittle. (*To* JIMMY.) You were laid up last year with that wrist. I won't have you falling.

JIMMY. That wasn't falling. That was opening a bottle of bubbly.

DAVIS. Champagne?

IRIS. Only for the anniversary. We don't drink it as a rule.

DAVIS. Anniversary?

SONNY. The very first time we appeared together in the West End, Mr Davis dear. February the sixteenth, nineteen twenty-four. It was the opening night of *Dancing With Daisy*.

JIMMY. We were in the chorus.

IRIS. You have to start in the chorus. You'll find that.

DAVIS. I was telling Miss Terralozzi. The vicar was asking if you'd do a turn at the Senior Citizens.

IRIS. Go out?

DAVIS. There's a Gala Evening for the new premises.

IRIS. We don't go out.

SONNY. We would, Mr Davis dear. We would. But we don't.

ROSE. We don't like going out.

JIMMY. Not out of doors.

DAVIS. Miss Terralozzi said the fee wasn't big enough for artistes of your stature.

Pause. They turn away from him.
In the big room:

JOHNNY. He's had more than his time, Lil. They'll be missing him at the shop. Won't do much good teaching him dramatic movement, if he gets the old heave-ho.

JOHNNY *comes into the passage.*

Ding dong! Ding dong! School's out.

The others react to his voice. Overlapping dialogue: 'Johnny.'

To DAVIS: 'It's Johnny.' 'Johnny's back.' JOHNNY *goes on in.*

Morning Mr Davis. I saw Mr Simon as I came by the shop. He was standing in the doorway, looking worried.

DAVIS (*quick look at watch*). I'm late.

ROSE. Johnny's not wearing a hat.

DAVIS. We've been doing dramatic movement.

ROSE. Where's your hat, Johnny? Did you take it off?

DAVIS. If you've got a hat, I'll take it with me, if you like.

JOHNNY *shakes his head. They are all watching.*

Or anything in that line.

JOHNNY. Nothing in that line. You cut along now, eh, old son? Tell Mr Simon I kept you, if you like. On a business matter.

DAVIS. That's right, Mr Sims: I shan't get into trouble. (*Moves into the passage.*) Don't worry about me. It's hard to get assistants these days. He has to give me the latitude. (*Calls.*) Goodbye, Miss Terralozzi. Thank you.

LILY (*calls*). Come again on Thursday.

DAVIS. Thursday.

LILY. I shall be stronger.

DAVIS. Thursday, then. (*Going.*) Goodbye, all. (*He has gone.*)

SONNY. Such a sweet boy!

IRIS. Nothing, Johnny?

JOHNNY. Not a sausage.

SONNY. It's not sausages we need, Johnny dear. It's bowler hats.

JIMMY. I wouldn't mind a sausage. I haven't had a sausage for a long time.

SONNY. Or a good-class umbrella.

IRIS. Despatch case. If it's real leather.

JIMMY. Can we go in to the fire now? (*As they go.*) I'd fancy a sausage. Chipolatas. I often think of them.

General move towards the fire in the other room.

LILY. Johnny was not successful. He had ill fortune.

IRIS. He's told us.

JOHNNY. I got some mags, you know. And the papers.

ROSE. (*looks for them.*) Oh, he got the magazines.

IRIS. You should have taken the Bakerloo Line. I keep telling you, but you won't listen. You're obstinate, Johnny.

JIMMY. He should have gone back to East Acton. There was that bag of groceries at East Acton.

IRIS. Lightning never strikes twice in the same place. Stanmore, Dollis Hill, Wembley – it's a wealthy area: you could get anything there. Gloves ... chiffon scarves ... handbags ...

JOHNNY. I don't like handbags.

SONNY. They're not lucky for you, Johnny dear. Not handbags. Remember when you sat on that handbag all the way from Tufnell Park to Tooting, and there was nothing in it but a bus ticket?

IRIS. There was no need to sit that long. He wasn't hatching it. (*To* JOHNNY.) You were nervous: that's all.

JOHNNY. I don't like handbags, Iris. It feels like stealing.

ROSE (*has found the bundle*). Did you get me *The Lady*, Johnny?

IRIS. Did you get the *Reader's Digest*?

ROSE. I was reading the advertisements. There's a lovely guest-house in Ilfracombe. Refined religious family with cream teas. (*Finds a magazine, and sits.*)

LILY. I won't have Iris reading the *Digest*. She gets notions.

SONNY (*looking through the magazines*). I just take the *Standard*, dear. Unless you've got anything in *my* line, Johnny dear. (JOHNNY *shakes his head.*) I once found a book of artistic poses inside a bush in Holland Park, but that was in the old days. You never get them left in the tube.

ROSE. What are we going to do for the anniversary? Sonny was saying champagne.

IRIS. He can take the Bakerloo tomorrow.

ROSE. There's not much time.

JOHNNY. Iris, I can't take the Bakerloo. Not first thing. I've got to be in the City at ten thirty.

LILY. I told that boy your work took you to the City.

JOHNNY. Lil, he knows. (*Spreads underground diagram on the table for* IRIS.) Look, old girl, Kennington at eight thirty, right? Fourpenny ticket. North to Euston.

IRIS. You don't need to go to Euston. You could take the Bakerloo to Wembley.

JOHNNY. Not so *early*, Iris. North to Euston. Back to Warren Street ... Goodge Street: you get the shop assistants at Heals, leaving their knitting.

IRIS. Sonny never did finish that knitting.

SONNY. I couldn't, dear. I didn't have the pattern.

JOHNNY. *There's* your gloves – Goodge Street, Tottenham Court Road, Leicester Square – across to Piccadilly Circus, Oxford Circus – there's your Liberty scarves. Then the Central Line to the City – bowler hats, umbrellas, brief-cases, *The Investors' Chronicle*. (IRIS *grunts*.) There's no latitude until eleven o'clock. After that, you can make a choice.

IRIS. You didn't have to choose the District Line. There's money in Bushey.

JOHNNY. It's a long way, Iris. Bushey ... Watford ... it takes all morning. Anyway it's swings and roundabouts, old girl. People are more careless in Ladbroke Grove than they are in Watford.

IRIS. And what do you get in Ladbroke Grove? Curry powder and green peppers. We've got to have something to sell.

JOHNNY. Well, I'm sorry.

JIMMY. Johnny ... What are we going to do, then?

IRIS. Johnny must go out again.

LILY. I won't have Johnny under pressure.

IRIS. We are under pressure.

SONNY (*is reading the paper*). Oooh! Very saucy!

LILY. What?

SONNY. Nothing, Lily dear. Just an advert. Just reading the Personal Column.

ROSE (*looks over his shoulder*). Let me see. (*Tries.*) Hold it higher. I can't read.

IRIS. If you won't wear glasses, what do you expect?

JOHNNY. What is it, Rosie?

ROSE (*reads*). 'Life-in-Death. Preserve your Loved Ones and We Will Pay. Limited Offer Only.'

LILY. Americans!

ROSE. No, no, Lily. It's in the *Standard*.

LILY. Give it to me. (*Takes the paper: business with her spectacles. Reads.*) There! 'From London, Ohio, to London, England. Knight's Embalming Service Brings Life-in-Death to the British People.' Of course it's Americans. Who else could it be?

JOHNNY. What's Life-in-death?

LILY (*looks*). Embalming. Filthy habit. (*Paper back to* SONNY.)

SONNY. 'With Life-in-Death Even the Remotest Relatives May Pay Their Last Respects Without Offensive Odours.'

ROSE. Odours?

SONNY. Stops you going bad, dear. (*Reads.*) 'Lead-lined Coffins Allow Loved Ones to Look Their Best When Meeting Their Maker on That Final Day.'

JOHNNY. What did it mean? – they'll *pay*.

SONNY. Wait a minute: I'm trying to find it. (*Finds it.*) Oh, it's a school. They're running a school to train people to do it, and they need bodies. Fifteen pounds each. (*Looks up.*) There you are, Johnny dear, if you could find a body on the Bakerloo, we'd have ever such a nice anniversary.

JOHNNY. I suppose we couldn't . . .

IRIS. What?

JOHNNY. Postpone the anniversary? (*They all look at him.*) Have it later?

Pause.

LILY. Johnny, my dear, it *wasn't* later.

IRIS. February the sixteenth.

ROSE (*breaks down and begins to cry*). Nineteen twenty-four.

General concern.

SONNY. Rosie, dear!

IRIS. Rose!

ROSE (*weeping*). I can't help it. Just thinking of it. I was so pretty. I was always the pretty one.

SONNY. You *are* the pretty one, dear. You're the pretty one, and Iris is the handsome one –

LILY. And *I* am the beautiful one. Go to her, Jimmy. Johnny, console her.

JIMMY *goes to* ROSE, *and stands by her, helpless.* JOHNNY *pats her head.*

JOHNNY. There there, eh? There there, dammit!

ROSE. I was a little butterfly. A little moth. (*Indignant to* JOHNNY.) We've got the coldest room in the house, and now you say we can't have the anniversary party.

JOHNNY. I didn't say we couldn't have it. Just postpone it.

SONNY. It's not the same, Johnny dear. If you start letting things slide, you end up with nothing. It's not the time to speak of it, dear, but we have all made sacrifices.

JIMMY. That's right.

SONNY. If I'd played my cards right, if I hadn't been loyal and true to my friends –

IRIS. He wanted to keep you, that man. That's all.

SONNY. I could have been someone, dear.

IRIS. You'd have been kept.

SONNY. I'd have had chances made for me, Iris dear. Opportunities of all sorts.

She snorts.

But I was loyal, dear. I wouldn't break us up.

IRIS (*to* JOHNNY). You can't postpone it.

LILY. That will do, Iris.

IRIS. Well, we can't.

LILY. *I* shall tell my husband what he can and can't do, if you don't mind. (*To* JOHNNY.) You can't postpone it. An anniversary is on the day, or it is nothing. One doesn't postpone Christmas. One keeps it on the day Christ chose to be born.

SONNY. We'll have to pawn something.

JOHNNY. What?

Pause.

IRIS. There's the coffee lace.

LILY. Out of the question.

IRIS. We pawned it before.

LILY. Once. In the most dire emergency.

IRIS. It's an emergency now.

LILY. You're too quick, Miss Fellowes. You're too quick with the property of others.

SONNY. Share and share alike, Lily dear.

LILY. I will share a great deal, Sonny. I shall not share my clothes.

JOHNNY. We got twelve pounds for it before, my dear.

JIMMY. We could buy a lot with twelve pounds. We could buy sausages . . . a pie . . .

ROSE. Champagne.

LILY. I will not pawn my coffee lace for your anniversary.

SONNY. *Our* anniversary, dear.

Pause.

JOHNNY. We did get twelve quid, Lil. He gives more when he knows we're going to redeem it.

JIMMY. That's right.

JOHNNY. Last time we had it out again within the week.

LILY. That was ten years ago. Our circumstances have changed.

IRIS. If Johnny wasn't so nervous with handbags, we shouldn't be in this position.

JOHNNY. I won't go to prison, Iris.

IRIS. You don't like to be seen carrying one; that's all. You're afraid of what people might think.

LILY. Johnny is not to go to prison. He is not to be put at risk. I must remind you, Miss Fellowes, that my husband is the business manager here. He has always looked after us. We depend on him. I remind you of that.

Pause.

SONNY. Iris dear, Johnny's been very good to us. He's always looked after the money side, dear, first when he had it, and even after his own father had that little accident with the revolver, it didn't make any difference – Johnny went out to work, and we never wanted. And getting the money for our own act, and looking after the bookings, and touring with us, dear, all over Fourteenth Army, playing percussion which he'd never been used to. And even now, dear, he's got his own way of doing things; you've got to give him the discretion. If he doesn't like handbags, he doesn't like them.

ROSE. You ought to apologize to Johnny. He works very hard.

JIMMY. We wouldn't know what to do without Johnny, Iris.

Pause. IRIS *is ashamed, but defiant.*

IRIS. I won't apologize.

She leaves the room, and goes into the hall where she sits on the stairs. The others look at each other.

LILY. Sonny!

JOHNNY. No. I'll go. (*He goes to the hall.*)

LILY. Temperamental little thing!

JOHNNY *stands looking at* IRIS, *who won't look round.*

JOHNNY. Make it up, eh?

IRIS. I shan't say I'm sorry.

JOHNNY. Don't need to, old girl. We know it.

IRIS (*turns to him*). Oh, Johnny!

JOHNNY. Never been any good with handbags. I haven't the art of it, old girl.

IRIS. You should try . . . the Bakerloo.

JOHNNY. Try it tomorrow.

IRIS. There's money on the Bakerloo, Johnny.

JOHNNY. Come in now, eh? Come back to the fire.

IRIS. We'll have to pawn the coffee lace.

JOHNNY. She knows.

In the other room:

SONNY. It'll have to be the coffee lace, Lily dear. We all know it.

LILY. But what shall I wear?

SONNY. I'll think of something, dear.

IRIS *and* JOHNNY *return.*

Lily's decided to pawn the coffee lace, dear. You'd better take it round straight away. We've done a lot of work on that boy today. He ought to give us a good price.

JOHNNY. Thought I'd try the Bakerloo tomorrow.

LILY. If you take it now, Mr Davis will be alone in the shop.

JIMMY. Twelve quid we got last time.

SONNY. I hope he gives us more than that. You won't get much bubbly for twelve pounds.

LILY. We shall make the list while you are away, and you can visit the shops after your nap. (*She goes to the wardrobe, and takes out a very old-fashioned coffee-lace evening-dress on its hanger.*) Tell Mr Davis I shall require him to care for the dress while it is in his charge. (*Giving it.*) Impress on him, Johnny: he must take great care.

The bell rings. Pause. They look at each other. The bell rings again.

Go on, Johnny.

JOHNNY *gives the dress back to her, and goes into the hall to answer the door. The others listen.*

JOHNNY. Who is it?

DAVIS (*heard*). It's me. Mr Davis.

ROSE. Who? Who?

SONNY. It's Mr Davis, dear.

JOHNNY *has opened the door.*

DAVIS. The vicar dropped in.

LILY (*calls*). Johnny!

JOHNNY. Excuse me.

He goes back to the others. LILY *signs to him to close the door, and he does so. She gives him the dress.*

LILY. Strike while the iron is hot.

JOHNNY. Righty old ho.

He rejoins DAVIS. *Door left open.*

DAVIS. I came to tell you about the vicar.

LILY. Negotiate, Johnny. Negotiate.

DAVIS. The vicar said –

JOHNNY *takes him into the other room, closing the door.*

JOHNNY. No time for that now, old son.

DAVIS. He said –

JOHNNY. First things first. Got something for you here.

DAVIS. For me?

LILY. And now, Sonny, if you will get a paper and pencil, we shall make a list.

JOHNNY. Coffee lace. A good colour. Café au lait.

Pause.

DAVIS. It's been worn, of course.

JOHNNY. It's been worn to the opera.

DAVIS. Yes ... Worn.

JOHNNY. It's been worn before the Duchess of Kent, Mr Davis. Before Princess Marina, the Duchess of Kent.

In LILY's *room,* SONNY *is making a list.*

LILY. A glass of dry sherry before the meal. Champagne with.

ROSE. That's right, Sonny. I fancy a glass of sherry.

JIMMY. I haven't tasted sherry –

LILY. We had sherry in nineteen fifty-three. A glass of dry sherry before dinner. Each.

IRIS. The price has gone up. They raise it every year with the Budget.

SONNY. South African's cheaper dear. Or Australian. There was that lovely Australian we met in the war, doing one-night stands at Manipur Road. Digger, his name was.

LILY. I don't think anyone here would expect me to drink Australian sherry. And a roast of some sort. Beef or veal.

ROSE. Veal's a very *white* meat.

JIMMY. Veal's tasteless. You can't taste veal.

IRIS. Expensive. A leg of lamb; that's better.

LILY. Contrefilet de boeuf with roast potatoes and haricots verts. Write it down, Sonny.

SONNY (*writes*). Roast beef and beans ...

In the other room:

DAVIS. It's ten years older.

JOHNNY. Prices have gone up in ten years. You should give more.

DAVIS. It's had ten years' more wear.

JOHNNY. Nonsense! Once a year on the anniversary; that's all. It's in beautiful condition.

DAVIS. An evening dress – you want it new, Mr Sims. This is more than thirty years old, by your own account.

JOHNNY. We shall redeem it. Twenty-five pounds is nothing for a dress like that.

DAVIS. But how can you redeem twenty-five pounds? Not without some careless person leaves his wage packet in the tube.

Pause.

JOHNNY. Very well. Fifteen.

Making the list:

LILY. It's more than doubled in value. We shall allow thirty pounds to be safe.

IRIS. We can't spend thirty pounds on a meal. It's wicked.

ROSE. It's the Anniversary, Iris.

LILY. We've had a great deal more than thirty pounds spent on our meals before this. A great deal more, and by Johnny for one.

IRIS. Not lately.

ROSE. Johnny never stinted. Not when he had the money.

JIMMY. We should have that first supper again, Lily. That first one, when the waiter signed the menu. I'd like to have that again.

ROSE. That's right.

JIMMY. Johnny stood treat.

ROSE. Oh, he loved you then, Lily. He spent a lot.

LILY. He loves me now.

JIMMY: Oysters. We had a dozen oysters. I haven't tasted oysters –

LILY. With the champagne.

JIMMY. And beef.

LILY. Contrefilet de boeuf. As I suggested.

JIMMY. Roast beef. All bloody. That's what we had.

LILY. With burgundy. You'd better put down a bottle of burgundy, Sonny, and Johnny shall warm it by the fire. We're sure to finish the champagne with the oysters.

SONNY. But we're not having oysters.

LILY. Nonsense. Of course we're having oysters. Put down oysters. We can get the man at the fish-shop to come round and open them. Sonny. Read the list.

SONNY (*reads*). One bot Spanish sherry . . .

LILY. Dry.

SONNY. Dry. (*Reads.*) Two bots champagne.

IRIS. *Non*-vintage.

LILY: *dismissive gesture.*

SONNY. (*reads*). Six dozen oysters. One Hovis loaf. One pound butter. Three lemons. Three pounds fillet of beef. Three pounds potatoes. Pound and a half French beans.

IRIS. They're out of season.

LILY. They can be bought.

In the other room:

DAVIS. I'll give you four pound ten.

Pause.

JOHNNY. I can't tell them. It's too humiliating.

Making the list:

IRIS (*to* LILY). Anyway, I thought you had indigestion.

LILY. I have pains, Iris.

ROSE. In her upper stomach.

LILY. You know that.

IRIS. Wind!

SONNY. That's enough, Iris dear.

LILY. *Good* food is never indigestible. Oysters digest themselves. If you were more accustomed to high life, you would not need to be told.

In the other room:

DAVIS. But you could have a lovely anniversary for four pound ten. Bridge rolls. A bottle of wine. A chicken from Sainsbury's with roast and sprouts. After Eight mints. Nescafé Superior Brew with the Gold Label. You could have a spread. Get an ice-cream gâteau, and keep it on the window-sill; I've known that done. Stone's Ginger Wine for after-wards; it's warming. And half a bottle of whisky for a whisky Mac.

JOHNNY. It's not enough, Mr Davis. They're used to the best.

DAVIS. You could have the best. I came to tell you. There's no need to pawn Miss Terralozzi's effects.

JOHNNY. I don't understand you.

DAVIS. The vicar. You diverted me with the dress. He stopped by. We spoke. He appreciates your point of view.

JOHNNY. What point of view?

DAVIS. Eight and six. It's insulting to an artiste. He sees that. He's authorized me to increase the offer.

JOHNNY. For what?

DAVIS. Miss Terralozzi knows about it. They all do.
(*Opens the door.*) Excuse me. (*Crosses the hall.*)

JOHNNY *following.*

It's all right, Miss Terralozzi. The vicar says he can run to ten. Miss Fellowes, Mr Lynn, I've been in negotiation. It's two guineas each.

LILY. Johnny?

JOHNNY. I can't follow him.

LILY. What does he offer for the coffee lace?

JOHNNY. Four pound ten.

LILY. Insulting!

DAVIS. But I've got you ten guineas, Miss Terralozzi. I mean, if you want me to take the dress as well, that's extra. I wouldn't spend fifteen pound on food myself.

IRIS. Ten guineas for what?

DAVIS. The Senior Citizens. I told you.

Pause.

ROSE (*nervous*). We don't go out.

DAVIS. A professional appearance.

LILY. Tell him, Johnny.

JOHNNY. They don't go out, Mr Davis.

DAVIS. You said yourself, Mr Sims. You need the money.

SONNY. We never go out.

DAVIS. You're professionals.

IRIS. We've retired.

DAVIS (*desperate*). It's not fair.

JOHNNY. What?

DAVIS. You ask twenty-five pound for a dress not worth ten shillings. You go on at me about Princess Marina and the Duchess of Kent. You make me feel socially inferior, Mr Sims. And I've done my best for you. Miss Terralozzi said eight and six each was insulting. Well, I made representations for you. Out of my pure respect for you; I spoke very strongly. And all you can do –

JOHNNY. Mr Davis –

DAVIS. Spurn me; that's what you do. You spurn my endeavours.

Pause.

IRIS. We can't go out.

DAVIS. Why?

IRIS. Tell him.

LILY. After the war, Mr Davis, professional work was not easy to come by. We had been out of the country too long. People had taken advantage of our absence. Nevertheless we persisted.

IRIS. Crowd work.

ROSE. Table Service at the Corner House.

SONNY. Dressing.

JIMMY. Fairground employment.

LILY. But we kept the act together. Though they were not frequent, we still had bookings. We were never the top of the bill, you understand, but we had our own public; we had our style. The Three Posies, With Sonny and Jim. Mr Sims negotiated our contracts.

JOHNNY. Don't, Lil.

LILY. No one blames you, Johnny. No one here blames you.

DAVIS. You mean I should have let Mr Sims talk to the vicar?

LILY. We were approached by a Mr Wolf Flutter for an eight-week tour. It was an excellent offer, as it seemed. Mr Sims negotiated a fee. We were contracted. It was at a time – you would not remember it, of course, but ten years ago, there was something called Rock and Roll.

DAVIS. I've heard of it.

LILY. Our act was not of that sort. We made no concessions.

DAVIS. I understand that, Miss Terralozzi.

LILY. The other acts *were* of that sort.

DAVIS. You would have formed a contrast.

IRIS. We formed the bloody comic relief.

LILY. Thank you, Iris; I shall tell the story. (*To* DAVIS.) We had been hired, as we discovered, to be mocked by adolescents.

DAVIS. Teenagers.

LILY. If you prefer. On the opening night, finding the house difficult, we attempted to impose authority. We were unable to make ourselves heard. Personal expressions were used . . . Laughter . . . People attempted to climb on to the stage –

ROSE *begins to sob.*

Be quiet, Rose. (*To* DAVIS.) At the end of the week, since we were all distressed, Mr Sims approached Mr Wolf Flutter and asked him to release us from our contract. He refused. It was then we discovered that we had been engaged for this very purpose. To be mocked. (*Pause.*) We played the eight-week tour, Mr Davis, and for the latter part of the week it was twice nightly. (*Pause.*) We have not appeared professionally since then. We lack the confidence. Nor do we go out. We make our own entertainment. We have our own world here.

Pause.

Johnny, will you continue your negotiations for the dress?

DAVIS. I'll allow you five pound for the dress. (*Pause.*) I'm sorry. It's the highest I can go. (*He turns and leaves the room as:*)

The lights fade

The curtain falls

SCENE TWO

The curtain rises on a dark stage. We hear JIMMY *snoring.* IRIS *is making little moaning noises in her sleep. Hold this long enough to establish that each couple is in a double bed, asleep.*

In the room stage right, SONNY *wakes, gets out of his bed, looks in the dark for his slippers, puts them on, finds the overcoat at the back of the door, goes out into the corridor, switches on the corridor light. The overcoat is over long underwear and socks. He goes down the corridor and into the lavatory, closing the door behind him.*

IRIS. Sonny? ... Sonny? ... (*Realizes where he's gone.*) ... Oh ...

Loud snore from JIMMY *wakes* ROSE.

ROSE. Jimmy, you're snoring. Stop it, Jimmy. Turn over. Don't lie on your back. Oh dear! Oh dear! I never sleep. I never get a wink of sleep.

LILY *suddenly gives a loud cry. Silence. Then the lavatory door opens, and* SONNY *puts his head out.*

LILY *gives another cry, not so loud. Then noises at the back of the throat, as if she were fighting for breath.* JOHNNY *wakes, and sits up in bed.*

JOHNNY. What's the matter, Lil? What's up, eh? Indigestion?

More of the fighting-for-breath noises.

ROSE. What is it, Jimmy?
JOHNNY. I'll turn the light on.
ROSE. Turn the light on. What's happened?
JIMMY. Bad dream. Somebody having a dream.

LILY *gives another loud cry. Then she is dead.* JOHNNY *has got out of bed. As he reaches the light-switch by the door and switches on the light,* SONNY *goes back into the lavatory and pulls the chain. Then he returns to the corridor, and stands outside the door of the large room, uncertain whether to knock. While:*

JOHNNY. Lil? (*Goes to her.*) Lil? (*Pause.*) Lily, girl? (*Takes her hand.*) It's all right, girl. Nothing to worry. All gone now. (*Pause.*) Lily?

SONNY *knocks.*

What is it?

SONNY. Is everything all right, Johnny dear? Is Lily having a turn?

JOHNNY. I don't know. She doesn't speak.

SONNY *enters the room.*

I'll have to go for the doctor.

SONNY. You get dressed, Johnny. I'll stay with her.

(JOHNNY *is also wearing long underwear and socks. He takes his shirt and trousers from the back of a chair, and begins to put them on. Meanwhile* IRIS *has got out of bed. The women also wear underclothes in bed. She takes the second overcoat from the back of the door, and puts it on.*)

JOHNNY. She doesn't speak. She doesn't answer.

SONNY. She's had a turn, hasn't she? That's it.

IRIS *joins them.*

IRIS. Is it Lily?

SONNY. She's had a turn. It's her indigestion.

JOHNNY. It's her pains. She cried out. I turned the light on. I went to her. She doesn't answer.

IRIS *goes to* LILY *and takes her hand.*

Shall I get a glass of water?

IRIS. She's dead.

JOHNNY. What?

IRIS. She's dead, Johnny.

JOHNNY. But she was to have . . . tests. Tests for her pains.

IRIS. It was very quick, Johnny. It must have been very quick.

SONNY *gets a mirror from the dressing-table, and holds it to* LILY's *face.* JOHNNY *is watching him.* SONNY *looks across at* JOHNNY *after making the mirror test. Hold a moment between the two of them, looking at each other.*

SONNY. It's true, Johnny.

IRIS *crosses to the door, steps into the corridor, and calls upstairs.*

IRIS. Rose! Jimmy! Get dressed and come down. Lily's dead.

ROSE *and* JIMMY *sit up in bed.*

ROSE (*to* JIMMY). What? What did Iris say?
JIMMY. She said Lil's dead.
ROSE. She can't of died.
JIMMY. She could. We all could. We're old.
ROSE. She couldn't. It makes the numbers wrong.
JIMMY. Get dressed, Iris said. We're to go down.

They begin to dress, as IRIS *returns to the main room, and lights the fire.*

JOHNNY. I ought to go for the doctor.
SONNY. That's right. We'll stay here.
JOHNNY (*helpless*). They don't like to be called at night.
IRIS. You have to phone the doctor. That's the law. Have you got sixpence?

JOHNNY *feels in his pocket, and nods.*
    Go on, then.
JOHNNY (*hesitates*). You're sure . . . ? (*Takes a step towards the bed: cries out:*) Lil!

SONNY *takes his arm, and leads him into the corridor, getting* JOHNNY's *overcoat from the back of the door as they go, saying:*

SONNY. Go along, Johnny dear. You go and telephone. Give you something to do, dear. That's best.

JOHNNY *takes his coat, and goes outside. Meanwhile* IRIS *has lighted the gas fire. She moves across to the bed, and straightens the counterpane. She stays for a moment, looking down at* LILY's *body, her face blank.* SONNY *returns.*

IRIS. I never liked her, Sonny. Bossy interfering bitch! I'll miss her.

ROSE *and* JIMMY *have dressed, and come down into the corridor.*
ROSE. Iris?

SONNY. In here, dear.

ROSE *and* JIMMY *come in fearfully, each trying to push the other to go first, like two timid children.* ROSE *is delighted to discover that the fire has been lit.*

ROSE. You've lit the fire.
IRIS. Yes.
JIMMY. Johnny's gone out.
IRIS. To phone the doctor.

JIMMY *begins a curious half-sideways motion upstage. He wants to see the body, but he is afraid. He takes a quick peek.* IRIS *and* SONNY *watch.* ROSE *ignores him.*

Satisfied?
JIMMY (*comes to* ROSE). Lily's dead, Rosie.
ROSE. She can't die. I told you. It makes the numbers wrong. Lily's very strong. She's the strongest.
SONNY. It was her pains, dear. Her pains killed her.
ROSE. If everybody dies, I'll be left alone. She can't die.
JIMMY. I'll be with you, Rosie.
SONNY. That's right, Rosie. Jimmy'll look after you.
JIMMY. I'm very strong. I get hungry sometimes, but I've always been strong.
IRIS (*to* SONNY). We'll get dressed.

They go towards their own room. JIMMY *alarmed.*

JIMMY. You're not going to leave us alone with her.
IRIS. Somebody's got to stay with her.
SONNY. We'll leave our door open.

IRIS *and* SONNY *go into their own room, where they dress.* JIMMY *and* ROSE *look fearfully towards the body, and move a little further away from it.*

JIMMY. Johnny'll have to have our room. We'll have Iris and Sonny's room. They'll come in here.
ROSE. Ssssh!
JIMMY. Iris'll have to give the lessons, and I'll teach falling.

ROSE. Sssssh, Jimmy!

JIMMY. He'll be very cold. Poor Johnny! It's a cold room, Rosie.

ROSE. You don't know she can't hear you.

JIMMY. What?

ROSE. You don't know the dead can't hear. Nobody knows. She could have her spirit, listening.

JIMMY *looks at her, alarmed. Pause. Then he goes to the screen that encloses the kitchen area.*

JIMMY. Come and help me with this screen.

They move the screen so that it masks the bed. JOHNNY *comes in from outside. He watches them for a short while, unnoticed.*

JOHNNY. What are you doing?

JIMMY. We thought she'd like the privacy.

SONNY. Is that you, Johnny?

IRIS (*leaves her own room*). Is the doctor coming?

JOHNNY. He said, tomorrow morning.

IRIS. But she's dead.

SONNY (*joining them*). Is the doctor – ?

IRIS. Tomorrow morning.

SONNY. But she's –

JOHNNY. He said, if she's dead there's no hurry.

ROSE. What does he expect us to do? Sitting here with Lily dead!

SONNY. He wouldn't take her away, dear. They don't do that. He takes a look, and writes a certificate.

JOHNNY. I don't want her taken away. Not yet. It's not respectful. This is her room.

ROSE *and* JIMMY *exchange a look.*

JIMMY. Yes, it is.

JOHNNY. It's her own room while she's in it. I won't have Lily rushed.

ROSE. That's right. That's very right and proper.

JIMMY. Where are you going to sleep, Johnny?

IRIS. He'll sleep in the chair.

SONNY. Was it her pains, Johnny?

JOHNNY. Angina something. Chest pains. He was going to give her tests. He didn't tell her. He had to take the tests first, he said.

JIMMY. My father died of his chest. Asthma. He died in the fog.

ROSE. He died in the Chiswick Empire, your father.

JIMMY. They've pulled it down now.

JOHNNY. It was a heart attack.

JIMMY. No, it was asthma.

JOHNNY. She had a heart attack. She wouldn't suffer, he said. He'll make the arrangements in the morning.

SONNY. What arrangements?

IRIS. Undertaker.

ROSE (*starts to cry*). Poor Lily! Poor Lily!

She is in the chair, crying. JIMMY *looks helplessly at* JOHNNY *for guidance. Then he starts to cry as well.*

JOHNNY. Don't cry, Rose. Don't cry.

ROSE. Lily's dead! Poor Lily!

JIMMY (*bawling*). Lily's dead.

SONNY. Be quiet, Jimmy dear.

ROSE. She'll miss the anniversary.

JIMMY *bawls louder.*

She always loved the anniversary. Sitting there at the head of the table in her coffee lace. Now she'll miss it.

IRIS (*hard*). Well, she won't be the only one.

ROSE *and* JIMMY *stop crying at once.*

JIMMY. What?

IRIS. She won't be the only one. There won't *be* an anniversary.

JIMMY. Because of . . . (*Indicates the screen.*) Because it's not respectful, Iris?

JOHNNY (*troubled*). Lil wouldn't have wanted that.

IRIS. Because there'll be no money.

JIMMY. But we've got the money. Johnny got it for the coffee lace.

IRIS. We'll have to pay the undertaker.

Pause. They take it in.

ROSE. No anniversary?
IRIS. We've got to bury her.
JIMMY. No anniversary?
SONNY. Er . . .
JOHNNY. What?
SONNY. I had a thought.
IRIS. What thought?
SONNY. Just something I read, dear.

Pause. IRIS *realizes what* SONNY *has been thinking of.*

IRIS. No, Sonny, no!
SONNY. I never mentioned it. I never spoke my thought.
JOHNNY. What does he mean, Iris?
IRIS. Never mind.

Pause. ROSE *gets it.*

ROSE. Oooh! Yes, that's right.
IRIS. That's enough, Rose.
JOHNNY. Is it a secret! What are you – ?
JIMMY (*gets it*). It was in the paper. Sonny found it.
IRIS (*angry*). Be quiet!

Pause.

SONNY. You've got to think of the living, Iris. Lily always did.

Pause. JOHNNY *looks at each of them. Then he realizes what thought is in their minds.*

JOHNNY. No.

He is about to leave the room, but SONNY *stops him.*

SONNY. Lily always had large ideas. Oysters.
JIMMY. Roast beef.
ROSE. Champagne. She said, champagne.
SONNY. Get the paper, Jimmy dear.

As JIMMY *does so,* JOHNNY *turns to* IRIS *looking for reassurance.*

JOHNNY. Iris . . . ?

IRIS. Leave me out of it.

SONNY. When I think of all she hoped for! Green beans and cigars. (JIMMY *has given him the paper*.) Thank you, Jimmy dear. (*To* JOHNNY.) It was Lily started the anniversary, Johnny. It was her idea. She thought of it, and you paid for it.

JOHNNY. Yes.

JIMMY. If it'd been one of us passed away, what would Lily have done?

SONNY. No, Jimmy dear: that's the wrong way about. What would Lily want *for* us? What would *you* want, Johnny, if you'd passed away, dear? If the anniversary was coming, and you knew the opportunity, what would you want us to do?

ROSE. That's right.

Pause.

JOHNNY. Damn!

IRIS. It's different for Johnny. Johnny's always sacrificed himself for us.

SONNY. I'd like Lily to have a nice funeral. It's the least we can do. What would it cost, Iris dear? What could we get for five pound? Lily always liked to make a good appearance. I've often heard her say that. Rolls Royces. Top hats. You wouldn't get your Rolls Royces, dear, for five pound. You wouldn't get your mutes and your black crepe. (*Turns to the advert: reads.*) 'A first-class headstone in glazed granite with appropriate remembrances hand-carved, and coloured granite chips to cover the grave.' (*Looks up: to* JOHNNY.) Chips! It's all included, Johnny. They include chips, dear.

Pause.

JOHNNY. You do what you want. I can't stop you.

SONNY. No, dear. You have to sign the form.

ROSE. Johnny's always looked after things. All the official things. Johnny manages us. We don't go out.

JOHNNY. Not this time.

SONNY. Do you think *we* didn't love her?

Pause.

JOHNNY. I know you did.

SONNY. All these years. We've had our share of quarrels, but we've stayed together, dear. We've had our laughs and our disagreements. We've split apart, and come together again, we've toured and we've shared, and we've stayed together. We've given up chances. We all have. Don't you think we didn't love her. She was one of us.

JOHNNY. I know you loved her. You don't need to remind me.

SONNY. And we love you too, Johnny. You do what *you* want.

JIMMY. She always liked the anniversary.

ROSE. She started it. Sonny said.

JOHNNY. Iris?

IRIS. Make up your own mind.

JOHNNY. But I've always . . . looked after you.

IRIS. Lily's told you what she wanted and you've done it. Now you've got to decide for yourself.

JOHNNY. You were artistic, and I looked after the practical side.

IRIS. You've been our slave for forty years.

Pause.

SONNY. That's not kind, dear.

IRIS. No, it's true.

SONNY. If you don't want the anniversary –

IRIS. I do want it.

JOHNNY. What?

IRIS. I do want it. It's what we live for. Something special once a year. Something to remember. But I want you to have respect, Johnny.

SONNY. He has respect.

JOHNNY. I have respect.

IRIS. No. We've relied on you. We've not respected you. You've not respected yourself. With selling Lily –

SONNY. With the embalmment.

IRIS. With selling Lily's body; that's what it is.

SONNY. With getting her a funeral, dear. A finer funeral than –

IRIS (*angry*). I don't care. I don't care what happens to Lily. She's dead.

ROSE. Iris, she might hear you.

JOHNNY. Eh?

IRIS (*more gentle*). No, Johnny, She can't hear. She can't tell
you what to do. She's dead. (*Pause.*) I always thought I didn't
like her, but now I miss her. And you loved her: I know that.
Working for her, working for us all, Johnny, you did it very
willing; I know that. How we bury her – it doesn't make any
difference to Lily. Selling her body to the Americans – that
won't hurt her. And if we have the anniversary or not – that
won't hurt her either. But you must do what *you* want,
Johnny. Decide for yourself, and have respect.

Pause.

JOHNNY. I can't change, Iris.

SONNY. Of course he won't. Johnny's been devoted to us all
his life, dear. He won't change now.

IRIS (*of the screen*). There's been a change.

JOHNNY. I have to think of what . . . she'd want.

SONNY. You know what she'd want, Johnny dear.

Pause.

IRIS. Yes, you know what she'd want.

JOHNNY. I've got the five pounds. We've not spent it. I'll go
to Mr Davis in the morning.

JIMMY. Eh?

JOHNNY. For the coffee lace, Jimmy. If she's going into the
hands of strangers, she must look her best.

Lights fade slowly.

*If the stage should have an apron, cross-fade to a pool of light,
stage left, and lower the curtain.* DAVIS *comes into the lit area,
carrying a large cardboard box.* JOHNNY *crosses in front of the
curtain from stage right. He gives* DAVIS *money, and takes the
box. Then he crosses back the way he has come. The light fades.
The curtain rises again. Screen is still round the bed, but* LILY *has
been put into the top of her coffee lace dress, and the others have
begun to make her up.*

*If there should be no apron, then this change should be done in a
twenty-second black-out. Try not to have to lower the curtain.*

IRIS. Jimmy, move the screen.

JIMMY *takes the screen away, as* SONNY *comes to look at what has been done.*

SONNY (*comes to them*). Very nice. Very tasteful and nice.

ROSE. Do you remember those eyelashes? Those were from *Lido Lady*. Lily never threw anything away. And the eye shadow's Meltonian Shoe Cream, because that's what Lady Lewisham uses. Meltonian Blue Suede.

IRIS. We'd better hurry. Johnny'll be back soon with the people.

ROSE. What about a beauty spot?

SONNY. Now there's an idea. That *is* a nice idea, Rosie.

ROSE. There's that little crescent moon she wore in *The Countess Mitzi*.

IRIS (*goes to the dressing-table*). I'll get it.

SONNY. On the cheek, Rosie dear, just below the bone, and put a little glitter on it.

JOHNNY *opens the door from outside to bring in* MADGE *and* MISS PEEL. MADGE *is dressed in a glamorized nurses's uniform,* MISS PEEL *is a temporary secretary.*

JOHNNY. In here. (*They are in the corridor*).

SONNY. It's them.

ROSE. But we're not ready.

IRIS. Jimmy, don't let them in.

ROSE. They're to wait till she's ready.

JIMMY *to the door. He halts the visitors in the corridor.*

JIMMY. Lily's not ready.

JOHNNY. Oh ... (*Looks at them.*) Er ...

MADGE. Lily?

JOHNNY. Miss Terralozzi. (*Corrects himself.*) Mrs Sims.

MADGE. But surely that's who – ?

JIMMY. That's right. She's dead, but she's not ready.

JOHNNY (*opens the door to* SONNY *and* IRIS's *room.*) If you'd like to wait in here, I'm sure she won't be long. (*Leads the way in.*) I'll put the fire on for you.

He plugs in the fire as they follow him in.

MADGE. I'm afraid I don't understand. Why isn't the – Why isn't your wife ready?

JIMMY (*from the door*). They're making her up.

JOHNNY. They're making her up.

JIMMY. Iris says she's to look her best.

JOHNNY. She has to look her best.

MADGE. But, Mr Sims, *we* do all that. It's part of the service.

JIMMY. I'll call you when she's ready. (*Shuts the door.*)

JOHNNY. Miss Terralozzi was an artiste. She didn't like the public to see her unless she was looking her best.

MISS PEEL. There's a girl where I live does underwater ballet at the Victoria Palace. She looks a right slut in the daytime, but she doesn't care who sees her.

JOHNNY. Yes. It wasn't like that in our time. Miss Terralozzi had very high professional standards. (*Going.*) Excuse me. I'm afraid the fire gives very little heat. It would be better not to remove your coats.

He goes into the next room. After MISS PEEL's *single exclamation, the action freezes.*

MISS PEEL. Well!

JOHNNY. Will you be long?

SONNY. We've done her neck and a beauty spot, dear.

JIMMY. What are they going to do, Johnny?

JOHNNY. They just want to have a look at her. Then I sign the papers, and get the money. Then they send a van to take her away.

IRIS. Well, they'll have to wait until she's ready.

In the other room.

MISS PEEL. It's creepy, your job, do you know that? It's a real creep.

MADGE. No, it's clinical.

MISS PEEL. What's the difference?

MADGE. The future's in embalming. It's the modern way.

MISS PEEL. I do shorthand and typing and answer the telephone: that's what I'm trained for, not to collect bodies.

MADGE. You don't have to collect anything. Just witness

identification and the signature of next of kin. We have an arrangement with Carter Patterson for collection. They give the vanmen black armbands, and charge extra.

In the other room LILY *is supported by* SONNY *and* ROSE *while* IRIS *is brushing her hair.*

JOHNNY. I'd better go back in.

IRIS. I won't be long. We'll send Jimmy in when she's ready.

JOHNNY. Yes . . . You've done very . . . she looks . . .

SONNY. She's the beautiful one, dear. She always was. And that dress was made for her.

JOHNNY (*going*). I'll go in.

SONNY (*as* JOHNNY *goes*). That dress was good enough for the Duchess of Kent, dear, so it ought to be good enough for God Almighty.

JOHNNY *crosses from one room to the other.*

MISS PEEL. You can earn more money as a temporary secretary. And I could never settle to anything. Seeing the same boring people, day after day. I mean, you've got to live.

JOHNNY (*has joined them*). She's nearly ready.

MISS PEEL. You ought to have two bars on this fire.

JOHNNY. We try to economize.

MADGE. I've got the papers here, Mr Sims, if you'd like to look at them.

She gets them and shows him.

It's a very simple form of contract. (*Points to the place.*) You see? 'In consideration . . .'

JOHNNY (*reads*). 'In . . . consideration . . .'

MADGE (*showing*). 'For purposes of demonstration only to bona fide students' – that's your guarantee against misuse.

JOHNNY (*reads*). 'Bona . . . fide . . .'

MADGE (*shows*). 'All student work to be under fully qualified supervision' . . . that's Mr Knight junior – Mr Lloyd Knight: he's got degrees in it from the Ohio State University.

JOHNNY. Yes.

MADGE (*shows*). 'To be prepared for interment in a first-class manner.'

JOHNNY. Interment?

MADGE. The funeral. First we leave a day for the lying-in-state, during which the near and dear may view and take their leave. Flowers are provided – whatever's seasonable and suitable – and there's continuous music of a reverential nature from a concealed source.

MISS PEEL. Frank Sinatra Sings Songs for Swinging Corpses.

MADGE. Please be quiet, Miss Peel, or I shall complain to the agency.

JIMMY *opens the door of the main room, and calls.*

JIMMY. Ready now.

JOHNNY. Where do I sign?

MADGE. Down here. Your full name, please.

JIMMY *has crossed the corridor and comes in.*

JIMMY. They've sent me. Lily's ready.

JOHNNY. I'm just signing the paper.

JIMMY. I'll tell them.

He returns to the main room.

JOHNNY. I haven't got a pen.

JIMMY. He's signing the paper.

ROSE. Does he want us?

SONNY. We'd better watch, dear. It's an important moment. Then we can bring them in to see her.

They join the visitors and JOHNNY *as:*

MADGE. Miss Peel, please get the presentation Gold Shaeffer from my briefcase.

MISS PEEL. The what?

MADGE. The pen.

MISS PEEL *gets the pen while others come in.*

JOHNNY. I'm going to sign with a gold pen.

JIMMY. When do we get the money?

MADGE. I have the cheque here.

JOHNNY. Cheque!

MADGE. Made out to cash, Mr Sims, as you requested.

JIMMY. There's not much time. You've got to do the shopping, and Iris'll cook.

MADGE *gives the pen to* JOHNNY.

MADGE. Over the stamp, please.

JOHNNY. All my names?

MADGE. Yes, please.

SONNY. He's got six, dear. Johnny's got six names.

ROSE. John Raymond . . .

JIMMY. . . . Howard Godolphin . . .

IRIS. . . . Destrange Sims.

SONNY. I hope there's room.

JOHNNY (*writing*). John . . . Raymond . . .

MADGE. I've been telling Mr Sims that Miss . . . his wife . . . will lie in state for twenty-four hours. We have a special Stateroom.

MISS PEEL. With seasonal flowers and reverential music.

JOHNNY (*writing*). . . . Howard . . . Godolphin.

MADGE. I'm sure you'll be most pleased and impressed when you see her.

SONNY. Oh, we shan't see her, dear. We don't go out.

JOHNNY (*writing*). . . . Destrange . . .

IRIS. Mr Sims will go. We don't go out.

JOHNNY (*stops*). What?

ROSE. Iris was just telling the people. We don't go out. You go out.

JOHNNY. But you'll go to see Lil lying in state?

Pause. All uncomfortable.

SONNY. We never go out, Johnny. You know that.

JOHNNY. You'll come to the funeral with me?

JIMMY (*to* MADGE). We've not been out for thirteen years. We don't go out at all, you see. Johnny goes out . . .

ROSE. We used to go out, but we don't go out now.

JOHNNY. But Lily . . . when they've . . . (*Looks to* MADGE *for words.*)

MADGE. Prepared her for interment in a first-class manner.

JOHNNY. When they've done that. When she's there in a lead-lined coffin for you to pay your last respects –

MADGE. . . . with padded silk interior, pink or blue, according to sex . . .

JOHNNY. You won't pay your respects?

Silence. Shiftiness.

You won't come to see Lil buried?

More silence. JOHNNY *stands up.*

You wanted me to decide for myself, Iris. I have. I'm not signing.

MADGE. Mr Sims!

JOHNNY. There's John Raymond Howard Godolphin Destrange on that paper but there's no Sims, and without Sims, it's not legal.

MADGE. No, it isn't.

SONNY. But, Johnny dear, they've brought the money.

JOHNNY. And *you* won't go out.

SONNY (*angry appeal*). We *can't* go out.

JOHNNY. And I won't sign. (*To* IRIS.) That's right, isn't it, Iris? For forty years, I've done what Lily wanted, what you all wanted. I was glad to do it. I played percussion, and looked after the business side, and went out every day in all weathers to find things in the underground, and I've taken them to Mr Davis, and we've lived on them. I've never done anything for myself or wanted to, only for Lily and for you. I've never taken a decision for myself, not for my own sake, and you've reproached me for it, Iris. I'm taking one now. (*To* SONNY.) You told me how much you loved Lily. Well, now you show me how much you loved her. You'll go to Lily's funeral, or I won't sign, and there'll be no money for an anniversary. (*To* JIMMY.) No turkey. (*To* ROSE.) No champagne. (*To them all.*) Lying-in-state with reverent music, I don't care about that, I'm not used to it; it can take care of itself. But you'll come with me to Lily's funeral, or I won't sign.

Long pause.

ROSE. I'll go, Johnny.

JIMMY. I'll go. We'll both go.

Pause. SONNY *looks at* IRIS.

SONNY. Well, *I* don't mind going out. I've always said we should go out more often.

JIMMY. Have you ? Then we'll all go out. We'll make a habit of it.

Pause.

IRIS. I won't go out.
She returns to the main room.

JOHNNY (*to the others.*) Well ?

SONNY. Come on.

He leads JIMMY *and* ROSE *across to where* IRIS *has her back to the door.*

MISS PEEL (*to* JOHNNY). My father was like you. That's why I left home.

ROSE. Iris!

JIMMY. Please, Iris!

SONNY. Iris dear, he won't sign without you go.

IRIS. No.

ROSE. But you started it.

JIMMY. You put it into his mind.

SONNY. Johnny never used to be like this.

IRIS. Lily wouldn't go out, and nor will I.

SONNY. Shut the door, Jimmy dear.

JIMMY, *surprised, does so.*

Iris, if Johnny leaves us, we'll *have* to go out. We mustn't make him angry, dear.

Pause.

JOHNNY. Excuse me.

He leaves MADGE *and* MISS PEEL, *crosses the corridor, and opens the door to the main room.*

Shutting the door, are you? (*Closes it behind him.*)

SONNY. Just a little conference, Johnny dear. Just something we wanted to say to Iris.

JOHNNY *goes to the bed, and looks down at the body.*

JOHNNY. She looks beautiful, Rosie. They (*Jerk of the head.*) won't make her look so nice, with all their chemicals.

ROSE. Do you like the beauty spot?

JOHNNY. It's the one she wore in *The Countess Mitzi.*

SONNY (*timid*). Iris did her hair, Johnny. Lily always had lovely hair, but it needed a lot of attention.

JOHNNY. Yes. (*Pause.*) Well, Iris? You wanted me to make my mind up, and now I have you don't like it.

IRIS. I've made mine up too. I'll not be forced to go out.

JOHNNY. Will you do it for love?

IRIS. That's not the point.

JOHNNY. But perhaps you didn't really want me to make up my own mind, old girl. Perhaps you just wanted to take Lil's place, and tell me what to do.

IRIS. I can't take Lily's place. I'm not your wife.

SONNY (*quick*). I'm not having the cold room, Johnny dear. Not with my kidneys.

JOHNNY. You'll have this room, you and Iris. I'll have the cold room.

IRIS. Lily wouldn't go out. She'd never go.

JOHNNY. Lily's dead. (*Pause.*) And I'm asking you to come with me and see her buried.

Pause. Then IRIS *crosses to the other room.*

IRIS. You can come in now. Mr Sims will sign.

SONNY *quickly arranges them in position so that the visitors can view the body.* IRIS *comes in with* MADGE. MISS PEEL *waits in the hall.*

JOHNNY. There's Lily. She's looking her best.

MADGE. What a pretty dress!

At this point, if the stage has no apron, the lights fade, the curtain falls, and the play ends.

If there should be an apron, cross-fade to the centre of the apron, and bring down the curtain. JOHNNY, ROSE, JIMMY *and* SONNY *can be heard, overlapping,* 'Mustn't be late. Mustn't be late.' 'This is Iris's coat.' 'This is Sonny's coat.' 'Who's got my coat?' SONNY, ROSE *and* JIMMY *come on downstage left to cross the front of the stage. They wear black armbands. They are a little timid. They look about them. The audience is treated as if they were people in the street.*

ROSE. It's so strange, Sonny, out in the street.
SONNY. It's been a long time.
JIMMY. It's cold.
ROSE. Where's Johnny? We can't go without Johnny.
JIMMY. There's a lot of people. More than there used to be.
SONNY. What do you expect, dear? There's more people all
    the time; it's natural.

JOHNNY *and* IRIS *come on, she with her arm in his.*

ROSE. Johnny dear, what a lot of people.
JOHNNY. Follow me, eh? Forward the Buffs.

They cross the stage, JOHNNY *and* IRIS, *then* SONNY, *then* ROSE *and* JIMMY. *As they're about to go off,* ROSE *lingers for a moment, looking into the audience.*

ROSE. Lovely people! Such nice people! We'd quite forgotten.

They go off. Stage empty. Lights fade.

Trevor

Little Boxes was first performed at the Hampstead Theatre Club on February 26th, 1968. The cast of *Trevor* was as follows:

JANE KEMPTON, *an upper-middle-class girl in her late twenties*
Anna Cropper
SARA LAWRENCE, *the same*
Angela Thorne
TREVOR, *a young actor, with traces of North Country in his speech*
David Cook
MRS LAWRENCE, *Sarah's mother, late fifties*
June Jago
MR LAWRENCE, *Sarah's father, the same*
Frank Middlemass
MRS KEMPTON, *Jane's mother, late fifties*
Maureen Pryor
MR KEMPTON, *Jane's father, the same*
Peter Howell
MR HUDSON, *the landlord, late fifties*
Larry Noble

On April 1st, 1968 *Little Boxes* transferred to the Duchess Theatre. The part of Sarah was there played by Elizabeth MacClennan.

The scene is the top-floor flat shared by Jane and Sarah.

Time: the present

We see the same set of rooms as we have already seen in THE
COFFEE LACE. *But this is a flat (two rooms, kitchen and bathroom) shared by a couple of young women in their late twenties,
both earning a good salary. It has been fairly recently decorated,
and the furniture, pictures and objects have been collected over the
last three years, so that they express a unity of taste in a pleasant
'Sunday Colour Magazine' way. Books. Record-player. Television. Indirect lighting. Central heating. Wall-to-wall carpets
in downstairs rooms and hall. A door-telephone set in the wall of
the hall by the door, and an ordinary telephone on a hall-table.
What was 'the cold room' in* THE COFFEE LACE *has become a
Habitat kitchen. What was the door to a rather squalid WC now
opens to a well-furnished bathroom. There is one rather odd aspect
of the set which will not be immediately obvious, but will appear –
what are normally a bedroom and living-room have been hastily
rearranged to look like two bed-sitters.*

The time is about 3.30 on a Saturday afternoon in February.
JANE *is lying on the studio-couch in the room at stage right,
smoking a cigarette and reading a book. A table is laid for tea –
cups and saucers, knives, forks and spoons, milk-jug, jam in a
pottery dish, butter in a saucer, a Fullers cake.*

The door from outside is opened by a latch-key. JANE *looks up
and listens.* SARAH *brings* TREVOR *into the hall.*

SARAH. Shall I take your coat?
TREVOR. What? ... Yes ... Thank you.

*She hangs up his coat together with her own, which she removes
without his help. While:*

SARAH. Straight in. It's the door on the left.

TREVOR *goes into the room stage left. He looks around, admiring
the room, and clearly a stranger to it. Having hung up the coats,*
SARAH *follows, closing the door behind her.*

TREVOR. You've got a nice place here.

SARAH. I share it with another girl.

TREVOR. You've each got your own room?

SARAH. Yes, and we share the kitchen and bathroom.

TREVOR. Where is she?

SARAH. She's gone out.

JANE *looks at her watch. Then she returns to reading.*

    Would you like a drink?

TREVOR. I'm not used to this.

SARAH. To what?

TREVOR. This . . . (*Gesture.*) luxury.

SARAH. Oh, really!

TREVOR. And I'm not used to being taken home by girls, as a matter of fact.

SARAH. Who usually takes you home?

TREVOR. That's not what I meant. (*Pause.*) Of course . . . my own place . . .

SARAH. Yes?

TREVOR. It's not much to take anyone back to.

SARAH. Why not?

TREVOR. I haven't got much money.

SARAH. Then why fritter it away, hanging around pubs?

TREVOR. You've got to do something.

SARAH. You could try work.

TREVOR. I told you; I'm an actor.

SARAH. Sorry. I forgot.

TREVOR. What do *you* do?

SARAH. I told you; I design fabrics.

TREVOR. That's right; you did. (*Pause.*) Shall we . . . (*Indicates studio-couch.*) I mean, do you want to sit down?

SARAH (*sits in a chair*). Thank you.

TREVOR *hovers, uncertain whether he is expected to share the chair with her.*

TREVOR. Shall I sit down with you?

SARAH. No.

Pause. JANE *looks up, looks at her watch again, half gets up, decides against it, and returns to reading.*

TREVOR. You're a funny girl.

SARAH. Why?

TREVOR. I mean, you picked *me* up. Standing there in your plastic mac, rubbing yourself up against me.

SARAH. I was not rubbing –

TREVOR. Asking me to come home with you.

SARAH. For a drink.

TREVOR. I thought you wanted to make all the running. Well, I didn't mind. Only now it looks as if I've got to do it. I'm not very good at that, as a matter of fact, because I'm a bit shy. I've got no instinct for it. I never know when it's time to put my hand on your leg – I mean, what the right moment is. Every girl I've ever been with has had to – sort of let me know – you know, tactfully – they move tactfully. I always have to know it's all right before I can go on to the next step.

SARAH (*rises*). I'll get you that drink.

TREVOR. Don't bother. I'm not much good if I've had too much to drink, as a matter of fact.

SARAH (*goes to drinks cupboard*). There's vodka and tonic.

TREVOR (*sits in the chair she's left*). Thank you.

JANE *looks at her watch again, gets up, opens her door cautiously, goes into the hall, and on up to the kitchen. From the cupboard, she takes a bowl and a packet of Scone Mix. She lights the oven. A buttered tin tray is already on the kitchen table. She starts to make scones. Meanwhile,* SARAH *has given* TREVOR *his drink – he thanks her – and goes to sit on the studio-couch, leaving* TREVOR *in the chair.* JANE *makes some slight noise in the kitchen.* TREVOR *hears it.*

What was that?

SARAH. What?

TREVOR. I thought I heard something.

SARAH. It's an old house. It makes noises.

TREVOR. Oh.

SARAH. Built by Gianino Pisco in 1824. You'll find it in *The A to Z of Historic London* if you're interested. Under P.

TREVOR. Ah.

Pause.

SARAH.   ⎫ Do you –
TREVOR.   ⎭ *You* aren't – *(Both stop.)*
SARAH. I'm sorry.
TREVOR. *You* aren't having a drink.
SARAH. No. I had more than I wanted in the pub.

Pause. He puts down his drink. There is another noise from the kitchen. He looks up, but SARAH *seems to have noticed nothing. He gets up, and goes towards her.*

  Don't *touch* me!
TREVOR. What?
SARAH. I don't want you to touch me.
TREVOR. I'm sorry.
SARAH. No, it's my fault. I'm sorry, Trevor. I'm very nervous.
TREVOR. My name's not Trevor.
SARAH. Never mind.
TREVOR. Why did you think I was called Trevor?
SARAH. It doesn't matter.
TREVOR. Did you go to that pub to meet someone called Trevor? Have you made a mistake?
SARAH. I did, and I haven't.
TREVOR. What?
SARAH. I did go to that pub to meet someone called Trevor, and I haven't made a mistake.
TREVOR. I don't understand you.
SARAH (*notices his slight accent*). You're from the north, aren't you? You're what they call a new wave actor.
TREVOR. Yes. There's a lot of us. That's why I'm not in work.
SARAH. Please sit down. Finish your drink. I'm sorry I snapped at you.

TREVOR *goes back to his chair.* JANE *puts the scones into the oven. Then she looks at her watch again, and comes back into the hall. While:*

TREVOR. I wish I knew what you're talking about.

JANE *hesitates, then enters the room stage left.*

JANE. Well?

SARAH. Trevor, this is Jane.

JANE. Have you told him?

SARAH. Not yet.

JANE. It's three forty-five. I've just put the scones in.

TREVOR. Er . . . (*He crosses his legs.*)

JANE. There's only half an hour.

SARAH. How long do they take? – The scones?

JANE. Don't worry about it. I'll see to it.

SARAH. Is there anything you want me to do?

JANE. No. I did it all while you were out.

TREVOR *crosses his legs the other way. They look at him, considering how to start.* JANE *begins.*

Trevor –

TREVOR. I'm sorry. I told your friend. My name's not Trevor.

JANE. Yes, it is.

TREVOR. She made a mistake.

SARAH (*to* JANE). He was on his own. He's an out-of-work actor. He needs money. I'm sorry about the accent, but a lot of people have accents now, you know they do.

JANE. The accent doesn't matter. If they take against him, they'll be all the more pleased when I break it off.

TREVOR. Look – (*Recrosses his legs uncomfortably.*)

JANE. Don't worry. We're just going to explain.

TREVOR. Then, if you wouldn't mind . . .

SARAH. Yes?

TREVOR. I mean, if it's going to take a bit of time –

JANE (*looks at watch*). It can't take much.

TREVOR. I had a lot of beer in that pub, and –

SARAH. It's at the end of the hall.

TREVOR (*gets up*). Thank you. (*He leaves the room and goes up the hall into the bathroom.*)

JANE. You took your time.

SARAH. It wasn't easy.

JANE. All you had to do was go up to someone and –

SARAH. You can't just approach a man like that. I had to stand there for hours, rubbing myself up against him.

JANE. Rubbing yourself up!

SARAH. Metaphorically. Then when we got back, he thought –

JANE. I know what he thought.

SARAH. Well, he was bound to. I had to discourage him.

Pause.

JANE. Love, I'm sorry. I am sorry, love. I was here ...
reading ... wondering.

SARAH. I know. I could feel you wondering all the way from
the pub. Wonder and jealousy. They were very thick on the
stairs when we came in.

JANE. Jealous! Of him?

SARAH. You'd be jealous of the *Manchester Guardian* if it was
delivered every day.

JANE. I'll tell him. I'll just put it to him. He can only say, No.

SARAH. I wish we didn't have to.

JANE. We do have to.

SARAH. Couldn't we say Trevor had a business conference or
something?

JANE. Script conference. My Trevor writes for television: do
try to remember. *Your* Trevor's in ICI.

SARAH. Sorry. Couldn't we say he had a script conference, and
couldn't get here? Then I'd ring up from a phone box, and
pretend to be him.

JANE *gives her a look.*

Well, they wouldn't hear my end of the conversation.

The WC is flushed in the bathroom. TREVOR *appears, and comes
down the hall, while:*

JANE. We'll have to do that anyway if he refuses.

TREVOR *returns.*

TREVOR. Who uses Arpège? I took some. I like using other
people's things: it's a kind of kleptomania. I thought I might
brush my teeth with your toothbrush, but I don't really
know you well enough, do I?

SARAH. I can smell the Arpège. It's very strong.

TREVOR. That's the trouble. When it belongs to somebody
else, I always put too much on.

JANE. Trevor –

TREVOR. I told you –

JANE. That's the first thing. You've got to get used to answering to the name.

TREVOR. Why?

JANE. Just listen. You're not very well off, are you?

TREVOR. No.

JANE. And you're an actor. (*To* SARAH.) That's a bonus, Sarah, getting an actor. It's worth the extra time. (*To* TREVOR.) We want you to act.

TREVOR. What in?

JANE. Just for this afternoon. My parents are coming to tea. They live in Paignton, and I hardly ever see them, but once a year they make a family tour – a weekend in Maidenhead with my married sister, during which they visit me, then up to Buxton to my brother –

SARAH. He's a mining engineer. You might have met him.

TREVOR. I'm from Bolton.

SARAH. It's all the north, isn't it?

JANE. Then back home. They'll be here in (*Looks at her watch.*) fifteen minutes. They must think you're my fiancé.

TREVOR. Where is your fiancé?

JANE. I haven't got a fiancé. But I'm twenty-seven. My parents think I should have one.

TREVOR (*to* SARAH). But why did *you* –

SARAH. I picked you up because Jane's a friend of mine. She had to get things ready here. Finding you was the best way to help her.

TREVOR (*to* JANE). But twenty-seven's nothing. People get engaged at any age.

JANE. That's what I tell my parents. But my mother is rather a bossy woman, Trevor. She doesn't want me to become a dried-up spinster, and she does want to see some positive evidence of my intention to avoid that. (*Pause.*) But don't worry. I shall certainly break it off. It won't come to anything.

SARAH. We thought if you played up your accent a bit, and took milk first in tea, and dribbled your scones, Jane's mother might break it off herself.

TREVOR. But why couldn't you get one of your own friends to do it?

JANE. We'll pay you five pounds for the afternoon. Do you agree?

Pause.

TREVOR. I see.

JANE. What do you see?

TREVOR. If this is a bed-sitter, where's the dressing table?

JANE. In the other room.

TREVOR. The bedroom?

Pause.

JANE. Yes. (*To* SARAH.) He's quick, isn't he? It must come from working in the theatre.

TREVOR (*to* SARAH). And *your* mother?

SARAH. My mother's the President of the local Liberal Party, and she runs the Welfare Clinic, and she does part-time teaching of retarded children. She doesn't care if I get married or not, but she says she'd like me to be sexually fulfilled. Consequently *my* Trevor is a married man who works for Shell.

JANE. ICI.

SARAH. ICI. (*To* TREVOR.) But you don't have to bother about *my* Trevor.

TREVOR. What a pity!

SARAH. Do you need work that badly?

TREVOR. I didn't mean that. I meant ... What a pity! I'm sorry.

JANE. We don't need your pity. Will you take the job?

The doorbell rings.

(*Looks at her watch.*) They're early. Quickly – Will you do it?

TREVOR. Yes.

JANE (*going*). Sarah, fill him in.

She goes to answer the door by the doorphone.

SARAH *hastily briefs* TREVOR.

SARAH. You're Trevor Hudson. You live
in Chelsea – quite near here – in
Paultons Square – a flat. Christ, I can't
remember the number. Never mind;
they won't ask. You're a staff-writer
for the BBC: that's why you never get
your name in the *Radio Times*. You do
research and linking bits for pro-
grammes about animals and the Common Market. You're writing a novel.
It takes you ages because you can
never think of the right words. You
had some poems published when you
were at the university.

JANE (*conversation
not really heard.
Mother? . . .
What? . . . I
can't hear – . . .
Oh! . . . Yes . . .
(Thinks.) I'm
sorry; the door
buzzer isn't
working. She'll
have to come
down.*

TREVOR. Which?

SARAH. Any you like.

TREVOR. Oxford, then. I did *Charley's Aunt* at Southport
two years ago.

JANE *returns, appalled.*

JANE. It's *your* parents.

SARAH. What?

JANE. It's your parents. They wanted to surprise you. I told
them the buzzer wasn't working. You'll have to go down and
let them in.

SARAH. Jesus! (*Going quickly.*) Fill him in. (*She runs into the
hall, and out through the door.*)

JANE. Trevor works for ICI. He's married.

TREVOR. What about the scones? Shouldn't we take them out
of the oven?

JANE (*looks at her watch*). Oh God! God! Come on!

*They go quickly upstairs to the kitchen to get the scones out of the
oven, while:*

Trevor has two children. Twins. They were an accident. He
doesn't like them much.

TREVOR. What's his name?

JANE. Hudson.

TREVOR. But that's –

JANE. They're both called Hudson. Both Trevors. Hers and mine.

TREVOR. Convenient.

JANE. It's the landlord's name.

TREVOR. Trevor?

JANE. Hudson. Trevor, do listen! Trevor's an economist. He –

TREVOR. What's the landlord's first name?

JANE. How do *I* know? Landlords don't have first names. Put the scones in that basket, and cover them with a napkin. I'd better make some more.

TREVOR. He's an economist?

JANE. Very brilliant and young. He was married at eighteen. That's where the twins came from. It was a shotgun wedding in the chapel of Dulwich College. He and Sarah met at the National Gallery one lunch-time. He picked her up in front of a Study of Small Children Being Mobbed by Apes.

TREVOR. He did?

JANE. No. *I* did.

Door from outside opens. SARAH *heard. Both react.*

SARAH. Go straight in.

MR and MRS LAWRENCE *enter.* SARAH *follows.*

  I'll take your coat, mother. It's the room on the left.

TREVOR. There they are.

JANE. You'd better take the scones down.

MRS LAWRENCE. I thought you said Trevor was here.

SARAH. He is.

MRS LAWRENCE *goes into* SARAH's *room.*

MRS LAWRENCE. No, he isn't.

TREVOR. Hey!

JANE. Yes?

TREVOR. What do I do when *your* parents come?

JANE. I'll have to tell them Trevor had a script conference.

TREVOR. I could drop in for a drink later.

JANE. *You* could?

TREVOR. Trevor could.

MRS LAWRENCE. He's not here, Sarah.

SARAH *joins her in the room, leaving* MR LAWRENCE *to hang up his coat, take his scarf off, etc.*

SARAH. Well, he should be. (*Calls from the door.*) Trevor!

TREVOR (*calls*). I'm in the kitchen, making some scones. (*He comes downstairs, carrying the scones in a basket, with a napkin over them.*)

In the kitchen, JANE *puts the kettle on and lays a tray for tea.* TREVOR *stops to speak to* MR LAWRENCE.

How do you do?

MR LAWRENCE. Very well, thank you.

TREVOR. Stock Market's recovering, I see.

MR LAWRENCE. What?

TREVOR. Stocks and shares. They're very buoyant.

MR LAWRENCE. Oh . . . Good.

TREVOR. You have to keep a sharp eye on the state of the market in my job. I'll take these in. (*He goes into* SARAH's *room with the scones.*)

MR LAWRENCE *has begun to get the full aroma of the Arpège. He gazes after* TREVOR, *and sniffs the air, surprised.*

Scones. Eat them while they're hot.

SARAH. Mother, this is Trevor.

TREVOR. How do you do? Your husband and I have just been discussing stocks and shares.

MRS LAWRENCE. I'm so glad to meet you, Trevor. I've heard a lot about you. (*To* SARAH.) Sarah dear, you're wearing a very heavy perfume. I didn't notice it when we came in.

TREVOR. No, it's me. I put too much on. (*Sudden thought.*) Oh my Gawd, I forgot the kettle. (*He goes swiftly out again, passing* MR LAWRENCE *at the door of the room, and on up the stairs into the kitchen.*)

MR *and* MRS LAWRENCE *look after him, and then at each other.*

MRS LAWRENCE. *That's* Trevor?

SARAH. I told you so, mother.

MRS LAWRENCE. My dear, I hope you haven't made a mistake.

SARAH. Don't be ridiculous.

MR LAWRENCE. What was that about stocks and shares?

SARAH. He takes an interest in them.

TREVOR *has reached the kitchen, and sees the kettle already on.*

TREVOR. Oh, you've done it. What about cups and saucers?
JANE. There's the tray. How's it going?
TREVOR. Early to say. I'm concentrating on making a good impression. No cake?
JANE. There's a cake in the other room. You'd better cut it in half.

TREVOR *gathers up the tray.*

TREVOR. I'll come back when it whistles.
JANE. No. Let Sarah do it.
TREVOR. Oh, I don't – (*Realizes* JANE *wants reassurance.*) Righty-ho. (*Ready to go downstairs.*) I'd start making those extra scones if I were you.

JANE *takes a packet of Scone Mix from the cupboard, and begins on the scones.*

MRS LAWRENCE. Now we *are* here, we can take you and Trevor out for the evening. Your father's brought his Barclaycard.
SARAH. But Trevor's married. He has a family in Blackheath.
MRS LAWRENCE. Then what's he doing here, baking scones?
SARAH. He comes round on Saturday afternoons sometimes.
MRS LAWRENCE. Don't be silly, Sarah. If you only had the afternoon, you'd spend it in bed, not up to your elbows in dough.
MR LAWRENCE. Steady on, Hetty.
SARAH. As a matter of fact, we –
MRS LAWRENCE. Don't say you've been. That bed's not even rumpled.
MR LAWRENCE. Hetty!
MRS LAWRENCE. I've no time for prudery about sex, Harold. You ought to know that, if anyone does.
MR LAWRENCE. I do, dear; I do.

TREVOR *comes in.*

MRS LAWRENCE. Trevor, my husband and I thought you and

Sarah might like to come out with us this evening. There was a Hungarian film in the Sunday papers.

TREVOR (*begins to set the table*). Hungarian?

SARAH (*helps*). I'll help you.

MRS LAWRENCE. We hardly ever see Hungarian films in Bury St Edmunds. If one has to come to London, one oughtn't to waste the trip. (*To* SARAH.) I've already taken your father round the Victoria and Albert Museum.

MR LAWRENCE. I'll sit down for a bit if I may, and take my shoes off.

MRS LAWRENCE. We'll see the six o'clock show, and have dinner afterwards. Then we'll be able to catch the 10.45 home. Harold, what did you do with the *Good Food Guide*? We'd better find somewhere to eat between King's Cross and the Curzon Cinema.

TREVOR. That'll be lovely.

SARAH. But Kathy's expecting you. (*Slight emphasis.*) At home.

TREVOR. Who? ... Oh, Kathy. Yes, that's right; Kathy's expecting me. I've got a wife and family. (*To* MR LAWRENCE.) Twins. But I don't like them very much. If it hadn't been for them, I wouldn't be married. It's hard to forgive a thing like that.

SARAH. You're not trying, are you?

TREVOR. I'd better get the cake. (*To* MRS LAWRENCE.) We're only having half a cake because Jane's expecting *her* parents.

Bell rings. JANE *hears it, and begins to come downstairs, leaving the scones on the baking tray.*

That's them now. (*He meets* JANE *in the hall.*) Getting the cake.

JANE. I haven't had time to put the scones in.

He goes on into the room stage right. JANE *answers the door phone. Overlapping:*

MRS LAWRENCE. Jane? That's the girl – ?	JANE. Mother? ... Do come up. Push the door when it buzzes.
SARAH. The girl I share with.	

MR LAWRENCE (*has his shoes off*). That's better. That's much better.

JANE *pushes the buzzer that lets people in downstairs.* TREVOR *fusses with cutting the cake in half and looking for another plate to put his half on. He finds one under a plant.*

MRS LAWRENCE. How do you get on with her? You never say.

SARAH. Oh, very well. We don't really see much of each other. She has her friends, and I have mine. She's engaged, as a matter of fact.

JANE *has the door open, and is looking down the stairs. Kettle whistles in the kitchen.*

TREVOR (*shouts*). Sarah, can you go?

SARAH. I won't be a moment, mother. (*She goes into the hall.*)

JANE *turns to her for a moment.* SARAH *takes* JANE'*s hand, and squeezes it, then goes quickly up into the kitchen.*

MRS LAWRENCE. There's something wrong with that young man.

MR LAWRENCE. Lots of men wear scent nowadays.

MRS LAWRENCE. If one's going to be somebody's mistress, it's not up to *him* to bake the scones. It's not the basis of a satisfactory relationship. I think we'd better find out a little more about him.

JANE *has turned to look after* SARAH. *Consequently her attention is off the door, through which* MRS KEMPTON *now comes sailing.*

MRS KEMPTON. Jane, dear!

JANE. Hullo, mother.

MRS KEMPTON *folds* JANE *in her arms, as* TREVOR *comes out of the room stage right with half a cake on the plant-plate.* MRS KEMPTON *drops* JANE *and advances to him.*

MRS KEMPTON. And you're Trevor.

TREVOR. Yes.

JANE. No! (*Moves behind her mother to sign to* TREVOR.)

TREVOR. Eh?

MRS KEMPTON *sniffs, and turns to* JANE.

MRS KEMPTON. Jane, you're wearing too much perfume.

TREVOR. No, it's me.

MRS KEMPTON. I beg your pardon.

TREVOR. I went a bit mad with the Arpège. Nerves, I expect. Knowing I was going to meet you.

JANE. Mother, you've made a mistake.

MRS KEMPTON. No, no, Jane dear, it's quite all right. (*To* TREVOR.) I understand.

JANE. No, you don't.

MRS KEMPTON. Trevor wished to make a good impression on his fiancée's parents, and accidentally put on too much after-shave lotion. That's not hard to understand.

As MR KEMPTON *appears, exhausted by the stairs.*

Harold, this is Trevor. (*To* TREVOR.) My husband takes longer to come upstairs than I because he likes to have a little rest on every landing.

TREVOR. How do you do, Mr ... er...

MR KEMPTON. How do! She ought to have a lift. You tell her. (*To* JANE). You ought to have a lift, Janey. Get one put in.

JANE. Mother, this isn't Trevor.

MRS KEMPTON. What?

JANE. This isn't Trevor.

MRS KEMPTON (*turns to* TREVOR). But –

TREVOR. Well ... maybe I'm not.

MRS KEMPTON. Then why did you say you were?

SARAH *comes downstairs from the kitchen with the teapot.*

SARAH. Trevor –

Stops dead as they all look at her.
Pause.

MRS KEMPTON. I don't know what's got into you, Jane.

SARAH. I'm so sorry. I interrupted.

MRS KEMPTON (*to* TREVOR). Are you Trevor or are you not?

TREVOR. Sort of Yes and No, in a manner of speaking.

JANE. Mother –

MRS KEMPTON. Just a minute, Jane. (*To* SARAH.) You're the girl my daughter shares the flat with. How do you do?

SARAH. Yes, I am. How do you do?

MRS KEMPTON. Sarah Lawrence.

SARAH. Yes. You're Mrs Kempton.

MRS KEMPTON. Exactly. (*Indicates* MR KEMPTON.) My husband.

MR KEMPTON. How do you do?

MRS KEMPTON. I know your name, Miss Lawrence. Little else. Jane writes very little about you.

SARAH. I'm sorry.

MRS KEMPTON. Don't apologize. You have your own life to lead; that's as it should be. Sharing a flat is a matter of convenience. I don't approve of close friendships between young women.

TREVOR. I'll just take the cake in.

MRS KEMPTON (*to* SARAH). You know Mr Hudson, of course?

SARAH. Trevor? Yes.

MRS KEMPTON. Thank you. (*To* TREVOR.) Take the cake in, Trevor, by all means. I shall join you in a moment. Jane dear, no doubt you wish to show me where to wash my hands. Harold, follow Trevor.

JANE (*indicates the door*). In here, mother.

TREVOR (*gives* SARAH *the cake*). For you.

SARAH *forestalls surprise in* MRS KEMPTON.

SARAH. My parents have come to tea unexpectedly. Trevor thought I ought to have half the cake.

MRS KEMPTON. Ah! ... I am glad my daughter bought one large enough.

JANE. This *way*, mother.

MRS KEMPTON *and* JANE *go into bathroom.* SARAH *and* TREVOR *look at* MR KEMPTON.

SARAH. Will you be coming in to say hullo to my parents?

TREVOR. I think I'd better, don't you?

SARAH. I'm sure you'd better.

TREVOR (*to* MR KEMPTON). Sarah's father's very interested in writing for television. We don't often get the chance to talk.

MR KEMPTON. Which is Jane's room?

TREVOR (*points*). That one.

MR KEMPTON. I'll just take my shoes off. We've been to see Queen Mary's dolls. My wife likes to keep active.

He goes into JANE's *room, sits, and takes his shoes off.*

SARAH. What happened?

TREVOR. She thought I was Jane's Trevor.

SARAH. So I gather. And Jane?

TREVOR. Wanted *you* to have me.

SARAH. Yes . . . Blast! I mucked it up.

TREVOR. Now you've both got me.

SARAH. But hardly both at once.

TREVOR. It's just like *The Corsican Brothers* I must say. I've always wanted to play twins. I'd better come in with you for a bit, and then get back to the others.

SARAH (*giving it*). Take the cake.

SARAH *opens the door and enters her own room.* TREVOR *following. As she sees him,* MRS LAWRENCE *says:*

MRS LAWRENCE. Trevor –

And at the same time the bathroom door opens and MRS KEMP-TON *comes out, and says:*

MRS KEMPTON. Trevor –

A frozen moment. Then the phone rings.

TREVOR (*gives* SARAH *the cake quickly*). I think it's for me. (*He answers the phone.*) Hullo? . . . What? . . . This is Trevor Hudson speaking. Yes, it's I.

Signs to JANE *who closes the door. Gives a conciliatory smile to* MRS KEMPTON. *Then, unseen by her, but seen by the audience if possible, cuts himself off from the caller at the other end, while continuing to speak.*

No, you tell Huw Wheldon I can't do it for that. He'll have to get Jonathan Miller . . . No, I'm sorry. Not a penny under two thousand . . . That's right. You tell him.

He puts down the phone, and his smile to MRS KEMPTON *is much more confident.*

I'm so sorry. Do forgive me. It's really not at all important, but my agent gets distraught if he doesn't know where to find me. Do please go in. Jane, did you put the kettle on?

JANE. No.

TREVOR. I'll do it. (*Opens the door for* MRS KEMPTON.) With you in a moment. I just want to whip up some scones to supplement the cake.

MRS KEMPTON. Whip?

TREVOR. Only a manner of speaking. Nothing kinky.

MRS KEMPTON *enters the room, giving another sniff at the reek of* TREVOR's *Arpège.* MR KEMPTON *looks up at her.*

MR KEMPTON. I thought I'd take my shoes off.

MRS KEMPTON. There's something odd about that young man.

MR KEMPTON. Oh, I don't know. Lots of men wear scent nowadays. I thought it was rather attractive.

MRS KEMPTON. That will do, Harold.

MR KEMPTON. He's a writer, isn't he? Bound to be artistic.

MRS KEMPTON. I don't want Jane getting into the newspapers. I think we'd better find out a little more about him. (*Looks around.*) Why isn't there a wardrobe in here?

TREVOR *has been leaning against the wall of the hall with his eyes closed, recovering, watched by* JANE.

JANE. Who was on the phone?

TREVOR. I don't know. Someone with asthma.

JANE. What?

TREVOR. Heavy breathing.

JANE. Oh . . . him.

TREVOR. You know him?

JANE. All the women in this district know him. He's called the Chelsea Breather. I usually put the phone down.

TREVOR. Well, let him breathe a bit next time. You owe him something. He saved my life. (*Moves.*) I'll get the scones in. That should give me a few minutes with Sarah's parents while they're baking. (*As he goes.*) I hope you noticed that two thousand quid's my minimum fee for scripts.

JANE. Yes. As far as my parents know, that's how much you make in a year.

TREVOR (*going*). Ah! . . . Well, you can't win them all.

JANE *goes in to her parents.* TREVOR *goes to the kitchen, and puts scones in the oven. He looks round for something to serve them on, and finds a plate and napkin. Meanwhile* SARAH *has been pouring tea for the* LAWRENCES, *handing scones, jam, butter, etc.*

MRS LAWRENCE. Where's Trevor?

SARAH. He had a phone call. Business.

MRS LAWRENCE. He's gone?

SARAH. No. He'll be in in a minute.

MR KEMPTON. Where's Trevor?

MRS KEMPTON. He had a phone call. Something about two thousand pounds.

MR KEMPTON. Good God!

MRS KEMPTON. He refused it.

MR LAWRENCE (*biting*). He makes a good scone.

SARAH. He enjoys cooking.

MRS LAWRENCE (*looks at* MR LAWRENCE). I suppose he doesn't get the opportunity at home.

SARAH. No, his wife does it all.

MRS LAWRENCE. Is that why he comes here?

SARAH. No, he comes to see me. As you know.

MRS KEMPTON. I suppose men's after-shaving lotion is designed to linger nowadays.

JANE. Why do you say that?

MRS KEMPTON. If Trevor shaved this morning, it's still rather strong.

JANE. It's not after-shave; it's scent. It belongs to Sarah. Trevor found it in the bathroom, and put some on just before you arrived.

MRS KEMPTON. Did he?

JANE. He told you; he was nervous.

MRS KEMPTON. It's all right, dear; I said I understood. (*Looks around.*) There's something odd about this room. I'll put my finger on it in a minute.

TREVOR *puts the scones in the oven and comes downstairs to join the* LAWRENCES, *going quietly past the* KEMPTONS' *door.*

TREVOR (*makes an entrance*). Everybody happy?

MRS LAWRENCE. What was your phone call?

TREVOR. Oh . . . financial matters.

MRS LAWRENCE. On Saturday afternoon?

TREVOR. Well, you know how it is.

MRS LAWRENCE. No, I don't.

MR LAWRENCE. I don't either.

SARAH. Trevor does a lot of free-lance work in his spare time.

TREVOR. That's right. I've got a wife and family to support.

SARAH. He's a consultant.

TREVOR. Yes.

SARAH. Firms consult him.

TREVOR. Always at it.

SARAH. He advises them.

TREVOR. They pay for my advice.

MRS LAWRENCE. He must be very brilliant.

TREVOR. Yes, I am.

MRS LAWRENCE. Tell me, Trevor, what exactly do you do at ICI?

Pause.

TREVOR. I'm glad you asked that question.

With the KEMPTONS:

MRS KEMPTON. Jane dear, how much do you really know about Trevor?

JANE. I've told you. He's a scriptwriter. He's –

MRS KEMPTON. We know what he does for a living; that's not the point.

JANE. What is the point?

MRS KEMPTON. How well do you really know him?

MR KEMPTON. Your mother's afraid he might be a nancy boy.

JANE. What?

MR KEMPTON. Homosexual. You know the sort of thing. Exposing himself in public lavatories.

JANE. Why?

MR KEMPTON. Just because he wears scent and likes cooking. I told her everybody wears scent these days. She said she didn't want you getting into the papers.

JANE (*to* MRS KEMPTON). You don't approve of my fiancé, mother?

MRS KEMPTON. I never said that. I just don't want you to rush into things and be sorry afterwards.

JANE. But you told me I ought to get married.

MRS KEMPTON. To the right man. Yes.

JANE. I wish you'd make your mind up. Last time, you said that at my age I couldn't afford to be choosy.

Pause.

MRS KEMPTON. He's a long time with the scones, dear. Do you think you ought to go and –

JANE. – see what he's up to? Don't worry, mother. He's hardly likely to be exposing himself in the kitchen.

TREVOR. And that's it really.

MRS LAWRENCE. It doesn't seem very clear to me.

SARAH. Of course it is, mother. It's quite clear.

MRS LAWRENCE. But *do* large commercial corporations work like that?

TREVOR. Of course they do. If you watched television as much as I do, you'd know they do.

MRS KEMPTON (*gets up*). He shouldn't be doing the cooking. It's not a man's job. I'll help him.

JANE. No.

MRS KEMPTON. It will give us the chance for a little talk. (*Opens the door.*) Trevor –

JANE. Mother, I said, No. (*At the door.*) I won't have you making Trevor nervous.

MRS KEMPTON. Really, Jane, what –

JANE. Trevor gets nervous very easily. I'll go.

She goes into the hall, closing the door firmly behind her.

MRS KEMPTON (*sitting*). I don't like this, Harold. I don't care for it at all.

MRS LAWRENCE. Was that someone calling?

SARAH. No, I don't think so.

MRS LAWRENCE. Somebody wanted Trevor. I heard them distinctly.

SARAH. Jane's parents are here. I told you.

MRS LAWRENCE. But what should they want with Trevor?

TREVOR. I give them advice sometimes. On financial matters.

JANE *has gone upstairs to the kitchen, looked for* TREVOR *and seen he isn't there. She comes downstairs into the hall, and hovers outside the bathroom door.*

JANE. Trevor?

MRS LAWRENCE. There!

SARAH. That was Jane.

MRS LAWRENCE. But why should Jane –

SARAH. Mother, don't be so suspicious of everything.

MRS LAWRENCE. Suspicious? I don't know what you mean. What is there to be suspicious about?

TREVOR (*to* SARAH). Don't you have a cat called Trevor?

SARAH (*angry*). No.

TREVOR. Just trying to be helpful.

JANE *still undecided, looks at door of* SARAH's *room, then smells the scones burning in the kitchen.*

JANE. Oh Christ! The scones!

MRS KEMPTON. What are they talking about up there? They're a very long time.

MR KEMPTON. Dammit, they're engaged.

MRS KEMPTON. He's supposed to be meeting us, not gossiping with Jane in the kitchen. Besides, I don't want Jane talking about me to that young man.

MR KEMPTON. She's obviously done that already. That's why he put on all that scent.

JANE *has shot upstairs to the kitchen, and taken the scones out of the oven. She puts them on the plate* TREVOR *has left out, and covers them with a napkin. While:*

TREVOR. I suppose I ought to say Hullo to Jane's parents. I mean, they might be a bit hurt if I ignored them.

SARAH. They're very fond of Trevor.

MRS LAWRENCE. I thought you said you saw very little of Jane.

SARAH. I don't see much of her. Trevor just happens to get on with her parents. He collects people.

TREVOR. I'm terribly good with older women. (*Going.*) Do excuse me. I shan't be a moment.

He crosses the hall, opens the door, and goes in to MR *and* MRS KEMPTON, *just missing* JANE *as she comes downstairs with the scones on a plate.*

TREVOR. I'm so sorry. The scones won't be a moment.

MRS KEMPTON. But where's Jane?

TREVOR. Jane?

MRS KEMPTON. She went to fetch you.

TREVOR. Did she? That's right: she did. (*To* MRS KEMPTON.) Jane went to fetch me.

MRS KEMPTON. Then where is she?

TREVOR. She hasn't come back yet.

JANE *hesitates, then knocks at* SARAH's *door, and goes in. She is surprised not to see* TREVOR.

JANE. Er ... (*Pause. All look at her.*) I ... er ...

MRS LAWRENCE. Are you looking for my daughter's lover?

MR LAWRENCE. Hetty!

JANE. No ... No ... I ... (*Scones.*) I just brought you these.

MRS LAWRENCE. But we have scones already.

JANE. These are hot.

MRS KEMPTON. And where are the scones?

TREVOR. Scones?

MRS KEMPTON. You went to 'whip them up'.

TREVOR (*door*). That's right. They're ready. I'll get them.

MRS KEMPTON. Can't Jane bring them?

TREVOR. Oh, she'll need a bit of help. My scones are terribly heavy.

He goes quickly into the hall, and up into the kitchen, sees JANE *isn't there, goes to take the scones out of the oven, and finds they're gone.*

JANE. Well ... I'd better get back.

SARAH. Thank you for the scones.

JANE. That's quite all right.

MR LAWRENCE (*eating one*). They're very good.

MRS LAWRENCE. I have a great deal of difficulty keeping my husband away from starchy foods.

JANE (*going*). I'm so glad to have met you, Mrs Lawrence.

MRS LAWRENCE. You will find Trevor with your parents. He is giving them advice on financial matters.

JANE *is out and crosses the hall.* TREVOR *has looked for Scone Mix, found none, and is haphazardly mixing flour, milk and eggs in the mixing bowl.* JANE *is surprised not to find* TREVOR *with her parents.*

MRS KEMPTON. And where is Trevor?

JANE. Trevor?

MR KEMPTON. He went to help you.

JANE. Oh . . . Trevor. He's making scones.

MRS KEMPTON. Again!

JANE. The first lot didn't take.

The phone rings. JANE *and* SARAH *both respond to it as a welcome diversion.*

JANE. I'll go.

SARAH. I'll go.

Both go into the hall, where TREVOR *is already on his way down to answer the phone. Pause. They look at each other. Both shut the doors to their rooms behind them. Phone still ringing.* TREVOR *picks it up, and holds it a moment.*

TREVOR. Just letting him breathe. (*Puts down phone.*)

SARAH. I can't keep it up.

TREVOR. *You* can't?

SARAH. We should never have started. It's ridiculous. Like a farce.

JANE. We can't tell them.

SARAH. I'm sick of it. I'm sick of deceit.

JANE. Love, we've started the deception. We have to go on. If they find out now –

TREVOR. That's right. If you hadn't invented *me*, you could just be two friends sharing a flat.

SARAH. Well, we've got to do something.

JANE. What?

TREVOR. If you could just get rid of one set of parents, we could manage.

JANE. How?

TREVOR. Unless you'd rather get rid of me. I don't mind suicide in a good cause. I've often thought of it.

Doors to both rooms are opened simultaneously. MRS KEMPTON *and* MRS LAWRENCE *have grown impatient.*

MRS KEMPTON. ⎫
                             ⎬ Who was –
MRS LAWRENCE. ⎭

MRS KEMPTON. I beg your pardon.

MRS LAWRENCE. Not at all. (*To* SARAH.) Who was it, dear?

TREVOR. Wrong number. (*Looks from one to another.*) Ah well, back to the kitchen.

MRS KEMPTON (*as he goes*). Why?

SARAH (*quickly*). Oh mother, I don't think you know Jane's mother. Mrs Kempton ... this is my mother.

MRS KEMPTON. How do you do?

MRS LAWRENCE. I'm so glad to meet you. (*To* SARAH.) Sarah, why did Trevor –

JANE. And *we* haven't really been introduced, have we? I brought you some scones just now, but we never really met.

SARAH. Mother, this is Jane.

MRS LAWRENCE. How do you do? I was just telling my daughter, she never mentions you. Though apparently Trevor –

JANE. We lead rather separate lives, I'm afraid.

MRS KEMPTON. I'm sure Mrs Lawrence understands that, Jane.

MRS LAWRENCE. Sarah tells me your daughter's engaged to be married.

MRS KEMPTON (*looks towards kitchen*). Yes, we –

SARAH (*jumps in almost hysterically*). And Mr Kempton, mother. You haven't met Mr Kempton.

MRS KEMPTON. Trevor –

SARAH (*waving through door*). Hullo, Mr Kempton! Hullo! This is my mother.

MR KEMPTON. What? ... What? ...

SARAH (*to* MRS KEMPTON). It's so nice to have met you. (*Pulling* MRS LAWRENCE *back into her own room.*) Come along, mother. Mustn't let the scones get cold.

MRS LAWRENCE (*as she goes*). Will Trevor be long?

MRS KEMPTON. Is that girl right in the head?

JANE. Of course she is.

MRS KEMPTON. There's no of course about it.

JANE. She's having ... rather a difficult love affair at the moment. It makes her nervous.

MRS KEMPTON. What did that woman mean?

JANE. What woman?

MRS KEMPTON. 'Will Trevor be long?'

JANE. Sarah's mother is not 'that woman', mother. Her name is Mrs Lawrence.

MRS KEMPTON. What did she mean: 'Will Trevor be long?'

JANE. You must have misheard her.

MRS KEMPTON. Nonsense. I hope she understands that Trevor –

JANE. He advises her husband on scripts. It's a free-lance thing he does.

MRS KEMPTON. But she didn't know you. She had to be introduced to you.

JANE. She knows Trevor. I ... (*Inventing.*) I met Trevor through Sarah.

MRS KEMPTON. Indeed!

JANE. She gave a party, and of course she had to ask me. Trevor was one of the guests.

MRS KEMPTON. But you told me you met Trevor at the National Gallery in front of a picture –

JANE (*outburst*). Mother, for God's sake will you stop questioning everything I say?

Pause.

MRS KEMPTON. I don't know what's got into you today.

She goes back into JANE's *room.* JANE *is left in the hall. She*

would like to join SARAH, *looks at the door to that room, takes
a step, but of course she can't go in. At this point,* TREVOR, *in
the kitchen, drops the mixing bowl and says, 'Blast!' Since
his arrival there, he has looked doubtfully at his mixture, lit the
oven, and kept himself unobtrusively occupied in scone prepar-
ation until this moment.* JANE *hears him, is undecided whether to
go up, but decides against, and follows her mother.* TREVOR
*picks the bowl off the floor, and attempts to roll out the mixture
which has got very sticky. While:*

SARAH. I'm sorry. I really can't bear Jane's mother.

MRS LAWRENCE. But –

SARAH. I don't want to talk about it. If you can't bear someone
you can't.

MR LAWRENCE. Where's Trevor?

SARAH. In the kitchen. Making –

MRS LAWRENCE (*holds up two brimming plates of scones*).
Scones?

SARAH. I don't know what he's making.

MRS LAWRENCE. Harold, go and find out.

SARAH. No. Leave Trevor alone.

MRS LAWRENCE. Run along, Harold.

SARAH. Why?

MRS LAWRENCE. Because I want to talk to you privately, dear.

Pause.

MR LAWRENCE (*to* SARAH). Back soon. (*Goes.*)

SARAH. Father, you've forgotten your shoes.

MR LAWRENCE (*in hall*). Can't get them on. My feet have
swollen.

As MR LAWRENCE *gets into hall, the phone rings*

SARAH. I'll go.

MRS LAWRENCE (*calls*). Answer it, Harold, will you?

She closes the door firmly. MR LAWRENCE *answers the phone:*

MR LAWRENCE. Hullo? . . . Hullo?

MRS KEMPTON. Harold dear, why don't you have a word with
Trevor?

MR KEMPTON. Eh?

JANE. What about?

MR LAWRENCE. Hullo? . . . Hullo? . . .

MRS KEMPTON. If you intend to marry Trevor, dear, then naturally your father ought to get to know him. In the kitchen, Harold.

MR KEMPTON. Oh . . . All right.

MR LAWRENCE. Speak up. What do you want? This is (*Looking.*) – one of those number things. Used to be Freemantle, but they changed it.

JANE. Why does father have to go. Trevor'll be back in a moment.

MRS KEMPTON. Because I want to have a little talk with you.

JANE. Why –

MRS KEMPTON (*straight over her*). And I don't want your father to be embarrassed.

MR LAWRENCE. Hullo? . . .

MR KEMPTON (*to* JANE). Back soon, Janie. (*Going*).

JANE. Father, you've forgotten your shoes.

MR KEMPTON. Never mind. (*Closes the door behind him.*)

MR LAWRENCE. Hullo? . . . (*Puts the phone down. Sees* MR KEMPTON.) Nobody there.

MR KEMPTON. Wrong number?

MR LAWRENCE. Don't know. He didn't say.

MR. KEMPTON. How do you know there was anybody there at all.

MR. LAWRENCE. Asthma.

TREVOR *puts the new tray of scones in the oven, and comes downstairs. Seeing the fathers, he tries to back but is spotted.*

MR. KEMPTON. There you are, young man. I was just coming to have a word with you.

MR LAWRENCE. So was I.

MR KEMPTON. Were you? Why?

TREVOR. *Were* you? Ah, you were. Yes, of course you were. You both were. But you won't both want to have a word with me at the same time, will you? No, you won't.

MR KEMPTON. My wife says we've got to get to know each other.

MR LAWRENCE (*puzzled*). But you do know each other.

TREVOR. Better. We should know each other better. We all should. Everyone should.

MR LAWRENCE. Trevor gives you advice.

MR KEMPTON. No, that's what he gives you.

MR LAWRENCE. He gives you advice about –

TREVOR. I give everyone advice. It's a fault. Can't mind my own business. Mr Kempton – Mr Lawrence. Mr Lawrence – Mr Kempton.

MR KEMPTON } (*together*). How do you do?
MR LAWRENCE }

TREVOR (*to* MR KEMPTON). I expect you'd like to go to the loo, wouldn't you?

MR KEMPTON. No, I wouldn't.

TREVOR. Your wife went. It's nice in there.

MR KEMPTON. No, I don't think so, thanks.

MR LAWRENCE. Wait a minute. There's something I don't understand.

TREVOR. Never miss an opportunity, because you don't know when you'll get another chance. Royalty do it. They're always doing it. And President de Gaulle and everybody.

MR KEMPTON. No, thanks.

TREVOR. You could be out walking. Any minute you'd pass a fountain. Or a mountain stream. Trickle, trickle! Imagine it.

MR KEMPTON. I said, no thank you.

TREVOR. They've got blue bleach in the cistern. It colours the bowl when you flush. You pull the chain, and the water goes zzzzzz.

MR LAWRENCE. My wife wanted me to find out what you were doing in the kitchen.

TREVOR. Making scones.

MR LAWRENCE. Again? Bit obsessional isn't it?

The phone rings.

MR KEMPTON (*to* TREVOR). That for you?

TREVOR. No. Why?

MR KEMPTON. Thought it might be another of your –

TREVOR. No. It isn't.

MR LAWRENCE. Probably that fellow with asthma.

TREVOR. The Chelsea Breather. (*To* MR KEMPTON.) It's someone who breathes.

MR KEMPTON. I'll take it, then. (*Picks the phone up.*) Hullo? . . . (*Listens then nods to the others.*) Now look here, breather –

MR LAWRENCE. My wife says you've got to understand these people.

MR KEMPTON. They need a shock. A sharp shock. (*Into the phone.*) Breather, you need a shock.

MR LAWRENCE. They did some experiments at the Howard League. Got a lot of them in a group, breathing at each other. Found they preferred that to using the phone.

MR KEMPTON (*into the phone*). You run along and find some other breathers. We've had enough of you here. We – Hah! (*To the others.*) Hung up. (*Phone down.*) We shan't hear from him again. What was that about scones? (*To* MR LAWRENCE.) He's always making scones, this fellow, but you never see any.

MR LAWRENCE. Never *see* any?

Phone rings.

MR KEMPTON. I'll leave it off. (*Does so.*)

TREVOR (*to* MR KEMPTON). Look, sir, whatever you wanted to chat about, it's probably a bit personal, isn't it? So (*Indicating the door.*) if Mr Lawrence wouldn't mind –

MR LAWRENCE. Oh, I can't go back in there.

Smoke has begun to emerge from the oven door.

TREVOR. Ah! . . . (*Turns to* MR KEMPTON.) Er . . .

MR KEMPTON. Nor can I.

TREVOR. Oh.

MR LAWRENCE. My wife sent me out of the room. I can't go back.

MR KEMPTON. So did mine. Wanted to have a heart-to-heart with Jane.

MR LAWRENCE. Mine wanted to have a heart-to-heart with Sarah.

TREVOR. What about? (*Quick second thoughts.*) Wait! Don't tell me.

MR KEMPTON. Can you smell anything burning?

TREVOR *sniffs. Then he returns to the kitchen, the other two following. Thick smoke from oven. He opens it, looks inside, then closes the door again, and turns the oven off.*

TREVOR. You have to watch them.

MR KEMPTON. No scones, eh?

MR LAWRENCE. You could have some of ours. We've got lots.

TREVOR. There's some brandy in the cupboard.

MR KEMPTON. Ah. Wonder which of the girls it belongs to.

MR LAWRENCE. Sarah wouldn't mind.

MR KEMPTON. Or Jane.

TREVOR. Let's have some. (*Getting the bottle.*) Where do they keep the glasses?

MR KEMPTON. If you don't know, who does?

TREVOR. How true! Of course, they're downstairs, aren't they in the – in Sarah's ... Jane's ...

MR LAWRENCE. What?

TREVOR. In the chiffonier.

MR KEMPTON (*finds them in the kitchen cupboard*). Here you are.

TREVOR. Oh, *those* glasses. (*Filling them.*) You don't mind it neat. (*Toasting.*) Cheers.

All drink.

I needed that.

MR KEMPTON. Must be a bit of a strain.

TREVOR. You don't know how much.

MR LAWRENCE. Meeting the parents.

TREVOR. Exactly.

MR KEMPTON. Silly business. Unnecessary.

TREVOR. Yes.

MR KEMPTON. What young people do nowadays; it's nothing to do with their parents.

TREVOR. No.

MR LAWRENCE. You can't get Sarah's mother to see that, though.

MR KEMPTON. Or Jane's.

MR LAWRENCE. If two people want to live together –

MR KEMPTON. Oh, I don't know about living together.

MR LAWRENCE (*to* TREVOR). Anyway, you're not living together.

MR KEMPTON. No, he's not.

TREVOR. No, I'm not.

MR LAWRENCE. But the point is, if you did want to, you'd do it. Please yourselves.

MR KEMPTON (*to* TREVOR). Would you?

MR LAWRENCE. Your love life is your own affair. Nothing to do with your parents. (*To* MR KEMPTON.) Our generation should stay out of it.

MR KEMPTON (*to* TREVOR). But you're not going to live together?

TREVOR. No, I'm not.

MR KEMPTON. Jane's not that kind of girl. I'm sure she's not.

TREVOR (*pouring*). Let's have another drink.

MR LAWRENCE. Jane?

MR KEMPTON. My daughter.

MR LAWRENCE. Oh, Jane! Well, Jane would move out, I assume.

MR KEMPTON. Why?

MR LAWRENCE. Well, you weren't thinking –

TREVOR. No, he wasn't.

MR KEMPTON. What?

TREVOR. You weren't thinking.

MR LAWRENCE. No, I didn't imagine Jane would stay here if you were living together. Even my wife isn't that broadminded.

MR KEMPTON. She wouldn't want to stay here. No room, for one thing.

MR LAWRENCE. Exactly.

MR KEMPTON. I don't understand this. (*To* TREVOR) You're not going to live together.

MR LAWRENCE. I don't see why *you're* so bothered, Kempton.

TREVOR. Cheers.

MR KEMPTON. ⎫
MR LAWRENCE. ⎭ Cheers.

MR LAWRENCE. Funny.

TREVOR. What is?

MR LAWRENCE. My wife thought you might be queer.

TREVOR. Queer?

MR LAWRENCE. You know ... homosexual. That kind of thing.

MR KEMPTON. A nance. So did my wife.

TREVOR. Oh, I don't think people say 'nance' nowadays, do they?

MR LAWRENCE. I told her everyone wears scent in 1968.

MR KEMPTON. I don't. Never have.

TREVOR. Don't you?

MR KEMPTON. I wouldn't mind, though. I like scent. I respond to it.

TREVOR (*shifts a little away uneasily*). Do you?

MR LAWRENCE. I've never been attracted to scent. Smell, yes. Not scent. Sweat. I've always found sweat attractive.

TREVOR (*wipes his hands nervously*). Let me fill your glass.

MR KEMPTON. My wife wears Yardley's Lavender. It's not the same.

MR LAWRENCE. My wife hardly sweats at all.

MR KEMPTON. Funny my wife thought you were a nance.

TREVOR. Hilarious.

MR KEMPTON. Cheers.

All drink.

MR LAWRENCE. Of course she used to sweat when she was younger. We went to Antibes for our honeymoon, and she sweated like a horse. Now she buys one of those roll-on deodorants.

Conversational focus shifts downstairs. The men continue to drink in the kitchen.

SARAH. This is ridiculous. I won't have this conversation.

MRS LAWRENCE. He's not at all suitable.

SARAH. Suitability's got nothing to do with it. I'm not

marrying him. You wanted me to be fulfilled. Well, I am fulfilled. Trevor fulfils me every Saturday afternoon, and now you're complaining.

MRS LAWRENCE. A man like that couldn't fulfil anyone.

SARAH. What do you want? – A blow-by-blow account?

MRS LAWRENCE. Sarah!

SARAH. That shocks you, doesn't it. But you're supposed to be unshockable, mother; you're the one that understands people. All my life you've told me to understand people, and now I'm understanding you.

MRS LAWRENCE. What's that supposed to mean?

SARAH. Try working it out. Why you've nagged at me to find a lover, and why you don't like it now I've found one.

TREVOR. If your feet have swollen, you could put them in the fridge.

MR LAWRENCE. Cheers.

TREVOR. ⎫
MR KEMPTON. ⎬ Cheers.

MRS LAWRENCE. I don't want you to be unhappy.

SARAH. Don't you?

MRS KEMPTON. I don't want you to be unhappy, Jane. A man like that –

JANE. Like that?

MRS KEMPTON. You know what I mean.

JANE. No. Tell me.

MRS KEMPTON. I don't say Trevor's . . . effeminate.

JANE. Then?

MRS KEMPTON. He's clearly unstable. He's not stable, dear. Not the sort of man you could rely on.

JANE. What if I'll settle for someone who'll rely on *me*?

MRS KEMPTON. Don't make debating points.

JANE. Damn you, mother. I've had enough.

MRS KEMPTON. What?

SARAH. I've had enough.

JANE. You come here, meet someone –

SARAH. – for the first time. You don't really know –

JANE. – a single bloody thing about him –

SARAH. – and in fifteen minutes –

JANE. – you've written him off.

SARAH. You tell me you're concerned about my future.

JANE. You don't give a damn for anyone but yourself.

SARAH. Just because Trevor wears scent –

JANE. – and bakes scones –

MRS KEMPTON. Jane! Please!

MRS LAWRENCE. Sarah!

SARAH. Oh, you're so broad-minded, mother, so under-standing –

JANE. Narrow-minded! Intolerant!

MRS LAWRENCE. But, Sarah, if you love him –

MRS KEMPTON. – if you really love him that's a different matter.

MRS LAWRENCE. If you're sure you love him.

Pause.

SARAH. What?

JANE. Oh . . .

MR KEMPTON. I'll tell my wife, 'You've got it all wrong', I'll say.

MR LAWRENCE. Yes, *I'll* say that. (*To* TREVOR.) Don't you worry. I'll have a word with her.

MR KEMPTON. 'He's not in the least queer. He's just a very obliging fellow.'

MR LAWRENCE. Cheers.

MR KEMPTON. ⎫
TREVOR. ⎭ Cheers.

JANE. I'm sorry. I got carried away.

SARAH. I got carried away, mother. I didn't mean to hurt you.

MRS LAWRENCE. No, no, dear. I've no right to interfere.

SARAH. I was cruel. I didn't mean –

MRS LAWRENCE. You did, dear.

SARAH. No.

MRS LAWRENCE. And you were right. I look at myself, and what do I see? Prurient curiosity. And jealousy afterwards. I'm ashamed, Sarah.

MRS KEMPTON. I've been a bossy woman all my life. Of course, your father encourages it.

JANE. But, mother –

MRS LAWRENCE. Hearing you defend Trevor, 'Lord, lord!' I thought, 'I've had the impertinence to talk to this girl about fulfilment!'

SARAH. But I didn't mean to defend him. I just lost my temper.

MRS KEMPTON. You wouldn't be my daughter if you didn't pick someone unsuitable to marry.

JANE. But, mother, if he *is* unsuitable –

MRS LAWRENCE. Your father used to be a very passionate man.

MRS LAWRENCE. I think she'd been reading the BO advertisements.

MRS LAWRENCE. I forgot who spoke to me about it.

MR LAWRENCE. I couldn't very well tell her, 'I *like* BO.'

MR KEMPTON. Cheers.

MR LAWRENCE. ⎫
TREVOR. ⎬ Cheers.

JANE. I'm trying to say, you may be right.

SARAH. I have had . . . doubts about Trevor.

JANE. If you really think I should give him up –

MRS KEMPTON. No, dear, no.

MRS LAWRENCE. No, Sarah. It's your own life.

SARAH. Perhaps if I didn't see him for a while –

JANE. If we tried a separation until I feel clearer in my mind.

SARAH. I could talk to him. If he really loves me –

JANE. – he'd want me to be certain of what I feel; I'm sure of that.

MRS LAWRENCE. Perhaps later . . .

SARAH. No, I'll do it now.

MRS LAWRENCE. He's still in the kitchen with your father.

MRS KEMPTON. Your father's talking to him in the kitchen.

JANE. Yes, that's right. (*Going*). I'll send daddy down.

SARAH (*going*). I shan't be long. I think it's better if he leaves straight away.

MRS LAWRENCE. Oh, my dear, if you're sure.

SARAH. I am.

JANE. I shan't bring Trevor back. He's bound to be a bit upset.

MRS KEMPTON. My brave girl!

Both girls go into the hall, closing doors behind them. Both mothers sigh exhausted sighs. Pause.

MR LAWRENCE. Cheers.
MR KEMPTON. Cheers.
TREVOR (*stands*). Excuse me.
JANE. I've promised to give him up.
SARAH. So have I.
JANE. I said I'd talk to him, and he'd leave right away.
SARAH. Have you got the five pounds?
JANE. In my bag.
SARAH. Oh, love! Love!

They kiss, as TREVOR *comes downstairs.*

JANE. Trevor –
TREVOR. I don't feel well.
SARAH. No!
TREVOR. I had a lot of beer in the pub. And then vodka. And I've been drinking brandy with your fathers. I feel very strange.
JANE. Get him into the bathroom.

As they do so.

You'll be all right, Trevor. You'll be all right.
TREVOR (*last words*). I'm not Trevor.

Upstairs the two fathers sip brandy.

MR LAWRENCE. Think he's all right?
MR KEMPTON. My wife doesn't care for him.
MR LAWRENCE. Looked a bit shaky, I thought.
MR KEMPTON. Oh . . . that. Probably not used to it.
MR LAWRENCE. Used to what?
MR KEMPTON. Drinking brandy in the afternoon. Got out of the habit.

The door to downstairs is opened with a latch-key. MR HUDSON *enters. He looks round, sees the phone is off the hook and replaces it censoriously. He looks about him, then crouches to peer through the keyhole of the door right.*

Tell you a devil for the brandy. Old Johnny Chinaman.

MR LAWRENCE. Johnny?

MR KEMPTON. Manner of speaking. Old Johnny Chink.

MR LAWRENCE. Ah!

MR KEMPTON. Used to see a lot of those fellows during the war. Chiang Kai-shek's fellows. Devils for brandy. They'd knock it back by the tumblerful. 'Banzai', they'd say –

MR LAWRENCE (*pouring*). Couldn't have been 'Banzai'.

MR KEMPTON. By George, you're right there. What *did* they say. I wonder? Neat brandy. Tigers for it. (*Raising his glass.*) Banzai.

MR LAWRENCE. Cheers.

MR KEMPTON. No, no, old boy. It was something Chinese. Something colloquial. You'd learn it off a record nowadays, but in my time we actually had to meet these fellows.

HUDSON *has been puzzled by what he's seen through the keyhole of* JANE'*s room. He has left that door, looked about him, and tried the door of* SARAH'*s room. Nobody there but an old woman on her own. Equally puzzling. Now there is a gurgle from* TREVOR *in the bathroom.*

JANE (*heard*). Get his head under water.

HUDSON *goes to the bathroom door, and peers through.*

MR LAWRENCE. I suppose he is all right. Trevor.

MR KEMPTON (*stands*). I'll go and see. I could do with a leak. Too much talk about fountains.

He descends the stairs, and sees HUDSON.

Ah, bit of a queue, is there?

HUDSON (*startled*). What?

MR KEMPTON. Bit of a queue. (*Notices the phone.*) That's funny. Thought I left it off. (*Takes it off again.*) I hope he won't be long in there. At my age, the old kidneys –

HUDSON You shouldn't leave the telephone off the hook.

MR KEMPTON. Why not?

HUDSON (*replaces it*). The Post Office don't like it.

MR KEMPTON. You're from the Post Office, are you?

HUDSON. Er –

MR KEMPTON. Thought I hadn't seen you before. (*Towards the bathroom.*) Tell you what; let's bang on the door. He might have passed out.

HUDSON. Who?

MR KEMPTON. I had to climb over a lavatory door once in Dehra Dun. Been knocking it back a bit with a friend of mine. Brother officer, you know. In he went, locked the door, never came out. Couldn't let him down, so over the top I went. It was pretty to see him lying there, curled around the bowl.

HUDSON. *Who* may have passed out?

MR KEMPTON. But it was rather difficult to explain to the brigadier, when we both came out together.

HUDSON. *Who* –

MR KEMPTON. You wouldn't know him. Lumley – Mahratha Light Infantry. Oh – in there? My daughter's fiancé.

MRS KEMPTON *opens the door to* JANE'S *room, and looks out.*

MRS KEMPTON. Harold, to whom are you talking?

MR KEMPTON. Fellow from the Post Office come in for a bit of a leak.

MRS KEMPTON. From the *Post Office!* In here?

MR KEMPTON (*to* HUDSON). By George, that's true. Just because you're in the government service, that doesn't give you the right to barge into a private flat every time you want to –

HUDSON. I am not –

MR KEMPTON. Bloody Trades Unions throwing their weight around again. Dammit, you've got pillar boxes for that sort of thing.

MRS KEMPTON. Why should a man from the Post Office –

MR KEMPTON. I'd left the phone off the hook. (*To* HUDSON.) Had to. One of those breathers kept ringing up. Dring! Dring! Couldn't hear yourself speak. He'll ring again in a minute.

HUDSON. No, he won't.

MRS KEMPTON. How did he get in?

MRS LAWRENCE *opens the door of* SARAH'S *room, and looks out.*

MRS LAWRENCE. Harold!

MR KEMPTON. Yes? (*Comes to her.*) How do you do? I'm Jane's father; I don't think we've met. And this is a man from the Post Office come in for a –

MRS KEMPTON. That will do, Harold.

MR KEMPTON (*goes on into* SARAH's *room*). You don't mind if I sit down? Not much point in standing around when you're not even first in the queue. (*Sits.*)

MRS LAWRENCE. I was calling my husband.

MR KEMPTON (*gets up*). Ah! (*Crosses to the door: calls.*) Lawrence, your wife wants you.

He returns to his seat. MR LAWRENCE *hears the call and stands.*

MR LAWRENCE. What?

MRS KEMPTON (*to* MRS LAWRENCE). I have been trying to discover how this man gained entry to the flat. (*To* HUDSON.) If you're from the Post Office, why aren't you in uniform?

HUDSON. I'm not from the Post Office.

MRS LAWRENCE. A burglar? (*To* MRS KEMPTON.) Is he a burglar?

HUDSON. I'm the landlord.

MR KEMPTON (*makes a discovery*). I say! Lots of scones here!

HUDSON. I came to put the phone back on the hook.

MR LAWRENCE *descends the stairs from the kitchen.*

MRS LAWRENCE. Harold, where is Trevor?

MR LAWRENCE. Kempton went to find out. (*Passing* HUDSON.) How do you do? (*Sees* MR KEMPTON.) Kempton, where's Trevor?

MR KEMPTON. Still in there. Probably passed out.

MR LAWRENCE (*joins him in the room*). You've found the scones, I see.

MR KEMPTON (*passing them*). Have one.

MR LAWRENCE. Not allowed. Tea?

MR KEMPTON. God, no.

MR LAWRENCE. Ah! You haven't . . . ?

MR KEMPTON. Not yet. I told you. He's still in there.

MRS LAWRENCE (*from the door*). Harold, this man says he's the landlord.

MR KEMPTON. How did he get in, then?

MRS LAWRENCE (*to* HUDSON). How did you –

HUDSON (*crosses her and comes into the room: indignant to* MR KEMPTON). I have a key. I let myself in. I have the right to do so. (*Looks round.*) And now I shall go.

MRS KEMPTON *joins* MRS LAWRENCE, *so that they bar his way back into the hall.*

MRS KEMPTON. There's no proof of that.

MR KEMPTON. That's right. He could be a damned thief, come sneaking in here, pretending he wants to use the loo. (*Stands.*) Come here, sneak thief; I'm going to search your pockets.

MRS LAWRENCE. He said he wanted to put the phone back on the hook.

MR KEMPTON. How did he know the phone was off the hook?

Pause. HUDSON *now uneasy.* MRS LAWRENCE *and* MRS KEMPTON *come into the room, so that he is surrounded.*

MRS KEMPTON. Well, my man?

MRS LAWRENCE. How did you know the phone was –

MR LAWRENCE. It *was* off, though.

MR KEMPTON. What?

MR LAWRENCE. I mean, he is right. The phone was off the hook.

MRS LAWRENCE. But how could he know that?

Pause.

HUDSON. I have . . . ways of knowing.

MR LAWRENCE. What ways?

HUDSON. Mind your own business.

Pause.

MR KEMPTON. By George, you're not the landlord at all; you're that breather. You've been ringing up and breathing at us, and when I took the phone off the hook, you couldn't bear it.

HUDSON. I'm the landlord. I have the keys. It's natural for me to be here.

MR KEMPTON. You stole them, you breather.

HUDSON. No.

MR LAWRENCE. I suppose he could be both.

MRS LAWRENCE. What, Harold?

MR LAWRENCE. Landlord and breather. He could be both.

Pause. MRS KEMPTON *closes the door of the room.*

MRS KEMPTON. Do you mean that a man who breathes at women on the telephone has the key to my daughter's flat?

Bathroom door opens. TREVOR, SARAH *and* JANE *come into the hall cautiously.*

SARAH. It's all right. There's nobody here.

HUDSON. But I never use it.

TREVOR. Shouldn't I say Goodbye to *anyone*?

JANE. No.

MRS KEMPTON. Never use it? Of course you use it. You're using it now.

JANE. Just go. Quietly. We'll explain.

TREVOR. It's so impolite. Both of me just creeping off like this.

HUDSON. Only because the telephone was off the hook.

SARAH. Goodbye, Trevor.

JANE. Good*bye*, Trevor.

TREVOR. Wait a sec. I forgot something.

He returns to the bathroom.

HUDSON. You can ask your daughters. I never come here.

TREVOR *flushes the* WC.

MR KEMPTON. By George, he's out. (*Quickly to the door.*) Excuse me.

HUDSON. But –

MR KEMPTON. No, old boy. You've forfeited your turn. (*Opens the door.*) Jane, there's a breather in here, says he's your landlord. (*Passing* TREVOR.) There you are, Trevor. Feeling better?

TREVOR. Much better.

MR KEMPTON. You took your time.

TREVOR. Sorry.

MR KEMPTON *into the bathroom, closing the door.*

SARAH. Trevor! Go!

MRS LAWRENCE (*looks through the open door*). Sarah dear, just come in for a moment, will you please? Oh, is Trevor going? Just a minute. I'll have a word with him.

SARAH. Mother, I've already had a word with him.

TREVOR. Yes, she has, and I quite understand. Goodbye, Mrs Lawrence. Goodbye, Sarah. Goodbye, Jane. (*He has the front door open.*)

MRS KEMPTON (*calls*). Is that Trevor?

TREVOR (*calls*). Goodbye, Mrs Kempton.

MRS KEMPTON (*comes into hall*). I'll have a word with him before he goes. (*To* JANE.) Go on in, Jane dear; I just want a word with Trevor.

MRS LAWRENCE. Run along, Sarah.

SARAH. Mother, you *don't* want a word with him.

MRS LAWRENCE. Just to show there are no hard feelings, dear.

JANE *and* SARAH *look at each other, and at* TREVOR. *Then they go into* SARAH's *room.* HUDSON *regards them piteously.*

HUDSON. There's been a mistake.

SARAH. Yes.

MRS KEMPTON *closes the door.*

MRS KEMPTON. Now, Trevor –

TREVOR. Please, please! I know what you both want to say.

MRS LAWRENCE. All *I* wanted to tell you –

TREVOR. No need to put it into words.

MRS KEMPTON. There are no hard feelings.

TREVOR. Just say goodbye. Believe me, I do understand. It's better.

MRS LAWRENCE (*to* MRS KEMPTON). No hard feelings?

MRS KEMPTON. None.

MRS LAWRENCE. But I have no hard feelings for Trevor. I'm the one with no hard feelings.

MRS KEMPTON. Why should *you* have no hard feelings?

TREVOR. Surely if neither of you has any hard feelings, there's no need to go on about it.

MRS LAWRENCE. Because Sarah is going to give him up.

MRS KEMPTON. No, no, my dear, Jane is going to give him up.

MRS LAWRENCE. Sarah's going to give the affair time to cool.

MRS KEMPTON. Jane wants to be certain what she feels for him.

TREVOR. Mrs Lawrence –

MRS KEMPTON. Trevor is Jane's fiancé, Mrs Lawrence.

TREVOR. Mrs Kempton –

MRS LAWRENCE. Trevor is Sarah's lover, Mrs Kempton.

Pause.

TREVOR. Anyway, if they're both going to give me up, there's no harm done, is there?

W C *flushed.* MR KEMPTON *comes out of the bathroom.*

MRS KEMPTON. Harold, take Trevor into Miss Lawrence's room.

MR KEMPTON. *Take* him?

TREVOR *looks from* MR KEMPTON *to the women, then closes the door.*

TREVOR. I'll come quietly.

He follows MR KEMPTON *into* SARAH'S *room.*

SARAH. They know?

TREVOR. Yes.

MR LAWRENCE. Hello, Trevor. We've caught your breather.

HUDSON. I do not breathe. I have a right to telephone my own tenants.

MR KEMPTON. I don't understand this.

MRS KEMPTON *and* MRS LAWRENCE *follow them in, closing the door.*

MRS KEMPTON. Now.

HUDSON. I am not obliged to explain to you. All my tenants are single women. I have a duty –

MRS KEMPTON. What is this person talking about?

HUDSON. I do not breathe at women.

MRS LAWRENCE. No time for that now. Well, Sarah?

MRS KEMPTON. Well, Jane?

MR LAWRENCE. What's up?

MR KEMPTON. Don't ask me.

SARAH. Mother's found out that Trevor's Jane's fiancé as well as my lover.

MR LAWRENCE. What?

MR KEMPTON. Steady on.

SARAH. He's single as well as married, and he works for the BBC as well as Shell.

JANE. ICI.

MRS KEMPTON. Mr Hudson –

HUDSON. My name's Hudson.

TREVOR. Not Trevor?

HUDSON. Wallace.

MRS KEMPTON. I'm waiting for an explanation.

JANE. We put him up to it.

MRS LAWRENCE. Why?

JANE. You wanted Sarah to have a lover. (*To* MRS KEMPTON.) You wanted me to be engaged. You both went on about it. We invented Trevor. Both of him. Then you wanted to meet him. Well, you only come up to London one day a year; it didn't seem too difficult. We couldn't know Sarah's parents would arrive on the same day.

MRS KEMPTON. But why?

HUDSON. You've moved the furniture. That wardrobe belongs in the bedroom.

MR LAWRENCE. I thought you said you never used your key.

MRS KEMPTON. The bedroom?

SARAH. We don't have two bed-sitters. We have a bedroom and a living-room. The two couches push together.

TREVOR. Sarah, love, enough's enough.

SARAH. No, I'm sick of it. I'm sick of deception.

JANE. Sarah!

SARAH. I told you. I'm sick of deception (*To* MRS LAWRENCE.) Jane and I live together, mother.

MRS LAWRENCE. Yes, dear. You share a flat.

SARAH. We *live* together. There isn't any Trevor. There's just Jane and me.

MRS KEMPTON. Yes, my dear; you told us. It was a stupid deception, but I'm sure your mother won't hold it against you.

SARAH. Jane, *tell* them.

JANE. Sarah means –

MRS KEMPTON. We know what she means, dear. You and Sarah share a flat.

SARAH. Yes.

MRS KEMPTON. Naturally you're friends –

SARAH. Yes, we are friends.

MRS KEMPTON (*riding on*). It would be very inconvenient if you weren't. And since you're both a little shy. (*To* MRS LAWRENCE.) Jane's always been shy.

MRS LAWRENCE. And Sarah. Ridiculous. Pathologically.

MRS KEMPTON. Naturally you're embarrassed that you've neither of you found a young man yet.

SARAH. Yet!

MRS KEMPTON. I blame myself. (*To* MRS LAWRENCE.) I push Jane too much; I know I do. I had to push her when she was a girl, or she'd never have done anything.

MRS LAWRENCE. They're a more puritanical generation now. We were very frank about sex in the thirties. Perhaps I'm too outspoken. I brought Sarah up on D. H. Lawrence.

MRS KEMPTON. Did you?

MRS LAWRENCE. So she invents a lover. Then she's ashamed.

MRS KEMPTON (*to* JANE). You chose to play a joke on us, my dear. Not in very good taste, but perhaps we deserved it.

SARAH. Daddy . . . Mr Kempton . . . do you believe this?

MR KEMPTON (*fiddling with shoes*). I can't get these shoes on.

MR LAWRENCE. They're mine.

MR KEMPTON. Oh, is that it?

He gives the shoes to MR LAWRENCE *who puts them on.*

MRS KEMPTON. I don't know whose particular friend Trevor happens to be.

SARAH. Nobody's. I picked him up in a pub.

MRS LAWRENCE. There! You do go out and meet people.

SARAH. We never go out.

MRS KEMPTON. Anyway, now you have met Trevor, I'm

sure you'll get to know each other better.

TREVOR. My name's not Trevor.

MRS LAWRENCE. You must bring him down to Bury St. Edmunds, Sarah.

MRS KEMPTON. Jane, you must bring him to Torquay. (*To* MR KEMPTON.) Harold!

MR KEMPTON *gets up.*

SARAH (*to* JANE). They're going. They won't listen.

MR KEMPTON (*kisses* JANE *awkwardly*). Bye, Janey . . . Er . . .

JANE. Yes?

MR KEMPTON *looks at his wife, then decides against what he was going to say.*

MR KEMPTON. I'll just get my shoes.

He goes into JANE'*s room, and puts them on.*

MRS KEMPTON. Will you get the coats, Jane?

SARAH. You don't want to know, then?

MRS KEMPTON. Goodbye, Sarah my dear. I'm so glad to have met you at last. (*To* MRS LAWRENCE.) Goodbye, Mrs Lawrence. (*To* MR LAWRENCE.) Goodbye.

She and JANE *go out into the hall, and* JANE *gets the coats.* MR KEMPTON *joins them.*

SARAH. Mother, you've been open-minded all your life. You've boasted of it. Your mind was so open, I used to fall in.

JANE. Here are your coats.

MRS KEMPTON *kisses her.* JANE *entirely unresponding.*

MRS KEMPTON. Goodbye, my dear. You know we always enjoy seeing you.

MR KEMPTON. Bye, Janey.

JANE. Goodbye, daddy.

MRS KEMPTON *opens the front door.*

MRS KEMPTON. You're such a silent sulky little thing when you're upset.

She goes, her husband following.

JANE. Goodbye, mother.

She remains, gazing after them, then closes the door, while:

SARAH. I was cruel to you just now, do you remember, when we were arguing about Trevor? I was nervous and hating everything, and I lost my temper. I mocked you for being unshockable, and always understanding people. I said you ought to understand yourself for a start. And you took it, mother. You shamed me by seeing what I saw, and accepting it. Now accept me.

MRS LAWRENCE. You overdramatize, dear. (*To* JANE, *who returns.*) Doesn't she overdramatize, Jane?

SARAH. Do you remember that Easter I didn't come home. Jane didn't go home either. We'd just met – picked each other up in the National Gallery.

MRS LAWRENCE. You met in the National Gallery?

TREVOR. In front of a picture of small children –

SARAH. We went away together that Easter, to a cottage near Cirencester. It was down a long muddy path. We took Jane's haversack, full of healthfood bread and salami and tins of stuffed vine leaves and a pheasant in jelly, and we bought eggs and cream from the farm. We'd lie in bed very late, and one of us would wash up while the other chopped wood for the fire, and we'd go for long walks in the afternoons. It was warm Spring weather. We walked through wild anemones and celandines, through primroses and bluebells and wild garlic. We hunted for fossils in the quarry. At night, we'd pile the fire high with wood, and sit in front of it, playing bezique and eating chocolates.

MRS LAWRENCE. We must get our coats.

SARAH. I'm trying to explain something to you, mother. I'm trying to get you to feel something.

MRS LAWRENCE. Sarah dear, you don't need to explain to me about friendship. It's very rare. (*To* JANE.) Real friends are very rare, and much to be prized. (*To* MR LAWRENCE.) Harold!

MR LAWRENCE (*stands*). Off now, are we?

SARAH. I wasn't talking about friendship, mother. I was talking about love. We made love.

MRS LAWRENCE. Goodbye, Jane. I'm so happy to have met you. (*Into the hall.*) Goodbye, Trevor.

MR LAWRENCE (*following*). Bye, Trevor . . . Jane . . .

TREVOR. Goodbye.

SARAH *follows her parents into the hall, as they get their coats.*

MRS LAWRENCE. If you do want to bring Trevor down for a weekend, dear, we've plenty of room.

SARAH. Mother, if you're going to understand people, you'd better begin with what they do in bed.

MRS LAWRENCE (*going*). Sarah, Sarah, *how* you exaggerate!

MR LAWRENCE (*going*). I like Trevor, you know. And your mother's quite come round to him.

They have gone. SARAH *returns to the others.*

SARAH. Oh . . .

Here follows the most extreme obscenity that the Lord Chamberlain will permit a British actress to say on the stage in the late nineteen sixties: whatever the word is, she says it several times.

TREVOR. What did you expect?

SARAH *sits in the armchair.*

JANE. Shut up, Trevor.

HUDSON. If I understand you . . .

JANE. Yes?

HUDSON. There will be no question of . . . young men.

JANE. What?

HUDSON. In the flat. Visiting. (*Looks at* TREVOR.) Well, they may visit. From time to time. But –

JANE. We have few visitors, and no young men. You understand correctly.

HUDSON. Ah! I let all my properties to single women, you see. I like to feel . . . in a fatherly relationship. One can do very little to discourage young men, but I dislike them visiting.

TREVOR. What *can* you do?

HUDSON. If there are too many, I don't renew the lease.

JANE. We shall be model tenants in that respect.

HUDSON. Thank you. You won't object if I . . . ring up from time to time? I shan't speak, of course.

JANE. We'll know who it is.

HUDSON. I'll say farewell then. Miss Kempton ... Miss
Lawrence ... Mr –

TREVOR. Goodbye.

HUDSON (*going*). I'll show myself out.

TREVOR (*as he goes*). You know your way.

HUDSON *goes. Pause.*

It's just us, then. (*Pause.*) Not my most successful per-
formance, I'm afraid.

JANE. It wasn't your fault.

TREVOR. They do know, you know.

JANE. Yes.

TREVOR. It's just that they don't want to put it into words.

JANE. No.

TREVOR. You can't blame them.

JANE. I don't.

TREVOR. Sarah does.

JANE. Yes.

Pause.

TREVOR. I don't suppose you'll be taking me down to Bury St
Edmunds. Or Torquay.

JANE. No.

TREVOR. Thank you for the five pounds.

JANE. You earned it.

TREVOR. No, really, I enjoyed – Well, I did enjoy it actually.
(*Pause.*) Shall I see you around? (*Pause.*) If you were
going out for a drink or anything. I'm often in that pub
when I'm not working.

SARAH. We don't go out, Trevor. We hardly ever go out.

Pause.

TREVOR. My name's not Trevor. (*He goes into the hall, and
out by the front door.*)

They listen to it close. JANE *sits on the arm of* SARAH's *chair,
and puts a hand round* SARAH's *shoulders. Lights fade leaving a
single box of hard, white light, then all front lights fade, leaving
them backlit. They are sitting very still. Hold it.*

The curtain falls.

Methuen's Modern Plays

Edited by John Cullen